"It's no secret I'm an In-N-Out fan. But I also love a great story. Reading Lynsi's book is like watching a poignant, generation-spanning film, complete with a nostalgic soundtrack. Post-World War II, a poor, hard-working couple imagines a burger joint that folks can *drive through*! Over the next seventy-five years, they and their children and grandchildren experience monumental triumphs and tragedies as they carry on the dream. God's redemptive work is front and center in this intimate account of one of fast food's first families."

—JIM DALY, PRESIDENT OF FOCUS ON THE FAMILY

"What an amazing book! So many valuable insights about faith, family, and business. Reading about Lynsi's passion for business and helping the less fortunate is inspiring—we need more of this in our world. Thank you for being an inspiration to so many."

—MANNY PACQUIAO, EIGHT-DIVISION WORLD CHAMPION BOXER

"Lynsi gives us the Ins and Outs of her heart—she's the real deal! Her willingness to lead authentically with vulnerability, humility, and conviction is inspiring. Wow!"

—BRAD FORMSMA, BESTSELLING AUTHOR OF *I LIKE GIVING* AND HOST OF *THE WOW FACTOR* PODCAST

"Less than 50 percent of American businesses survive past five years, and 0.0006 percent will see billion-dollar revenues while maintaining real customer satisfaction. In her new book, *The Ins-N-Outs of In-N-Out Burger*, Lynsi Snyder shares the inside secrets of what sets a business venture apart by telling the story of three generations of her family dedicated to quality, service, and unwavering core values. From key insights into their limited menu and refusal to franchise to behind-the-scenes anecdotes and interviews with In-N-Out associates, and a deep dive into the company's principles rooted in the family's Christian faith, this book is a tell-all for aspiring entrepreneurs or those who simply want to be inspired. Lynsi's personal story is captivating, and the passion and transparency of her journey through highs and lows is a testimony to God's grace and her grit to take life's lessons and use them to become a true servant leader in one of the most beloved fast-food chains in America."

—CHAD ROBICHAUX, BESTSELLING AUTHOR OF *SAVING AZIZ* AND FOUNDER OF THE MIGHTY OAKS FOUNDATION

"In two sittings I finished *The Ins-N-Outs of In-N-Out Burger*, a book that is not easy to put down. Lynsi Snyder chronicles the inspiring story of her family's business, now seventy-five years strong and getting stronger. Her voice throughout is instructive, encouraging, and ultimately hope-filled. And at times it is blunt, raw, and vulnerable. Such candor is in short supply these days by successful executives writing about their companies. But not Lynsi. She's an open book. I found this read to be stirring and refreshing, cover to cover. If you want to understand more about quality customer service, value-based business principles, or laser-like corporate focus, read this book. If you're curious about a family's three generations of excellence, grit, and ingenuity, read this book. If you've faced setbacks, felt overwhelmed, or confronted tragedy, read this book. When you turn its last page, you will not only thank Lynsi for writing *The Ins-N-Outs of In-N-Out Burger* but, if you're like me, you'll thank God for his grace that can renew us all."

—BARRY H. COREY, PhD, PRESIDENT OF BIOLA UNIVERSITY
AND AUTHOR OF *LOVE KINDNESS* AND *MAKE THE MOST OF IT*

THE INs-N-OUTs OF
IN-N-OUT BURGER

THE INs-N-OUTs OF
IN-N-OUT BURGER

THE INSIDE STORY OF CALIFORNIA'S FIRST DRIVE-THRU
AND HOW IT BECAME A BELOVED CULTURAL ICON

Lynsi Snyder

PRESIDENT, OWNER & GRANDDAUGHTER
OF THE FOUNDERS

NELSON
BOOKS

An Imprint of Thomas Nelson

Published in Nashville, Tennessee, by Nelson Books, an imprint of Thomas Nelson. Nelson Books and Thomas Nelson are registered trademarks of HarperCollins Christian Publishing, Inc.

Author is represented by Tom Dean, Literary Agent with A Drop of Ink, LLC, www.adropofink.pub.

Thomas Nelson titles may be purchased in bulk for educational, business, fundraising, or sales promotional use. For information, please email SpecialMarkets@ThomasNelson.com.

Unless otherwise noted, Scripture quotations are taken from the New King James Version®. Copyright © 1982 by Thomas Nelson. Used by permission. All rights reserved.

Scripture quotations marked ESV are taken from the ESV® Bible (The Holy Bible, English Standard Version®). Copyright © 2001 by Crossway, a publishing ministry of Good News Publishers. Used by permission. All rights reserved.

Scripture quotations marked NASB are taken from the New American Standard Bible® (NASB). Copyright © 1960, 1962, 1963, 1968, 1971, 1972, 1973, 1975, 1977, 1995, 2020 by The Lockman Foundation. Used by permission. www.lockman.org

Scripture quotations marked NIV are taken from The Holy Bible, New International Version®, NIV®. Copyright © 1973, 1978, 1984, 2011 by Biblica, Inc.® Used by permission of Zondervan. All rights reserved worldwide. www.Zondervan.com. The "NIV" and "New International Version" are trademarks registered in the United States Patent and Trademark Office by Biblica, Inc.®

Interior design by Kristen Sasamoto.

Any internet addresses, phone numbers, or company or product information printed in this book are offered as a resource and are not intended in any way to be or to imply an endorsement by Thomas Nelson, nor does Thomas Nelson vouch for the existence, content, or services of these sites, phone numbers, companies, or products beyond the life of this book.

ISBN 978-1-4002-4300-6 (ePub)
ISBN 978-1-4002-4299-3 (HC)

Library of Congress Control Number: 2023942653

Printed in the United States of America
23 24 25 26 27 LBC 6 5 4 3 2

I dedicate this book to my family that has gone ahead; I will forever hold on to the things that each one of you has said. I will try to make you proud and use my past failures to help others out. I will always look to God and his Good Book without a doubt. You were all so special and helped build this iconic place. Thank you times infinity, and in my heart you take up so much space.

To our customers: I dedicate this book to you! A thank-you for every smiling burger ever served still won't say enough. Without your loyalty and love we wouldn't be going strong today. You are and will always be our original number one! It's not a job to most of us, because serving you is fun.

To my In-N-Out family: I don't know where to start, but I want to thank you from the bottom of my heart. My family would be so proud of you and all your hard work year after year. I miss them so much, but I have you, and to my heart you are so dear. I love you and, yes, you are family. Without you we wouldn't be serving our number one, the customers you see!

All my love to my family here and gone!

CONTENTS

CONTENTS

THE RIGHT PLACE AT THE RIGHT TIME

MY NAME IS TOM EVANS, AND I'M NINETY-SIX YEARS OLD. I WAS IN-N-Out's first employee. I got hired in the 1940s and worked there many years. I loved every day!

In 1944, I quit high school and joined the navy to become a radioman. I was assigned to the submarine base at Pearl Harbor. After my discharge in 1946, I returned to high school, graduated, and attended a community college on the GI Bill. I fell in love, got married, and soon our first child was on the way. I needed work to support my family, and I overheard two fellows discussing employment. One mentioned that a hamburger stand on Garvey was looking for help. I wasted no time and got myself over there on the double!

With the usual apprehension of a job seeker, I approached a stocky fellow who greeted me with an enthusiastic smile and asked, "What would you like?"

I asked, "Do you have a job opening?"

He asked about my cooking experience. I told him, "I can cook and I'm a Navy veteran, married, with a child on the way. I need a job."

The man sized me up and said he'd have to talk to his business partner, but he would give me a trial run. He introduced himself as Harry. We shook hands and agreed on a start date. I returned to my car, relieved and excited to join the working class. It was April of 1949, and I was In-N-Out Burger's first helper. Today an employee is known as an associate.

On my first day I reported to work at noon. Harry handed me a paper hat, along with an apron and a safety pin to secure it. He showed me around the kitchen and explained the job. We worked together until about 4:30 p.m. when his business partner, Charlie Noddin, arrived and Harry introduced me.

Then Harry took a sheet of paper out of the cashbox, and Charlie started to call out numbers. Harry wrote down everything. Charlie put another cashbox in the drawer and closed it. I wondered what was happening and quickly learned it was the daily inventory, when Harry and Charlie counted every bun, meat patty, slice of cheese, French fry boat, coffee cup, and bottle of soda. (An inventory practice, I'm told, that's still carried on today—seventy-five years later!) Harry disappeared into the washroom with the cashbox and balanced the cash against the inventory. He returned shortly to tell Charlie how many burgers and fries he had sold during his shift, and then they went outside and briefly discussed the numbers and— probably—how I was working out.

Harry left, and I worked with Charlie until about nine o'clock. Charlie didn't work as smoothly as Harry, nor was he as congenial. He was a good man and cordial, but he lacked Harry's big smile and his unique way of greeting each customer with "What do ya say?" and "How ya doing?"

All went well over the next few days, and when I arrived for the Friday evening shift, I was surprised to see a young woman working fries. I'd assumed Harry, Charlie, and I were the only employees. But while pinning on my apron I met Esther, Harry's wife. Sometime later, I met Charlie's wife, Margaret, while she was working fries.

Eventually Harry and Charlie were satisfied that I could manage a shift alone. This meant I would be responsible for the money and inventory for that shift. In those days a shift consisted of working the night shift and the next day shift. They decided I would run the Tuesday night and Wednesday day shifts, an arrangement that gave each of them a day off every two weeks. I worked six days a week with a day off every Monday.

It's interesting to note that Harry and Charlie did not have it all figured out early on. They were learning as they went. For example, Harry hired a former navy cook named Cover Bond later that year. He was in his thirties and knew more about cooking than any of us. He was in a state of shock to learn they were using household kitchen utensils and encouraged Harry to buy commercial utensils—large spatulas, professional-grade carbon-steel chef's knives, and a stone to sharpen the blades.

Harry and Charlie may not have had every detail figured out, but what they did have figured out was how to provide a high-quality burger, fries, and drink at a great price. Back then an In-N-Out hamburger was twenty-five cents, fries were fifteen, and bottled drinks were a dime.

One afternoon Harry made himself a hamburger and showed it to me. "Look," he said, pointing to the hamburger, bun, spread, lettuce, tomato, and onion. "That's meat, bread, and a salad. For twenty-five cents you can buy a meal. If you add in a drink and fries, it costs fifty cents. That's a whole dinner for a half-dollar!"

Back then Baldwin Park, California, was a rural area, and sometimes business would be so slow on Tuesday evenings that it was hard to justify being there. Late one night a nearby farm brought unexpected business. I was working alone when a fellow drove up and asked if he could get fifty hamburgers.

That took my breath away. Fifty burgers!

"Sure," I said. "Are you having a party?"

"No," the farmer said. "We're picking tomatoes, and I have a crew to feed."

I asked, "Would you like some fries?"

He replied, "I'll take twenty."

One person making fifty burgers alone was a challenge, but I was up for it! Fortunately, I didn't have other customers until I finished the order. At the time, that was the largest single order ever. It may still be the largest order ever handled by one person.

As the weekend approached, the burger volume would begin to creep up on Thursdays, with Friday through Sunday accounting for over half the weekly business. Because of the scheduling, Harry worked every other Friday night and the Saturday day shift.

One day Harry mentioned that Charlie was selling more on his shift than he did. It irritated Harry that old Charlie could do that. Since I worked with both, I knew that Harry took orders and cooked faster than Charlie did. But no matter how hard Harry tried, Charlie remained ahead in this unspoken competition.

It's incorrect to say that Harry ever really took a day off. Even on his day off Harry was up at dawn, headed for the butcher to select the day's meat and have it ground. He'd check our supply of patties and make more if necessary. Each morning he cleaned the fryers, added the oil, hosed the floorboards, and swept and washed the floor. Harry believed we should always appear busy whether we had customers or not. He didn't want the helpers to be outside drinking coffee or having a smoke. So on Tuesday nights at about 10:30, with few cars on Garvey Avenue, I would put hot water in the sink, add a cleaning agent, and wash down the walls. Harry wanted the place spotless.

Harry was often annoyed that our fries sometimes cooked inconsistently. Usually they were crisp and brown, but other times they were greasy and limp. To figure out the problem, Harry paid a visit to Laura Scudder's, Southern California's foremost potato-chip maker at the time. They were sympathetic to Harry's plight and graciously took him on a tour of their facility, and Harry learned that the starch in potatoes converts to sugar, and sugary potatoes make limp fries. To keep potatoes starchy, they must be stored at a constant cool temperature. So Harry had a metal shed made for the potatoes and placed it at the end of the storage shed. The new setup let him buy potatoes in a larger quantity and get a better price.

Without a doubt, Harry was innovative. One day I found him on the driveway adjusting a recently installed box mounted on a metal post. There was a two-way speaker inside the box so we could talk to the customers without shouting back and forth to the cars! It was a first and Harry and Charlie established a trend—California's first drive-thru. The combination of the drive-thru and the two-way speaker system was such a hit that cars would often stop at the speaker just so they could use it instead of giving the order at the front window. At first, one downside to using the speaker was that it interrupted the cooking process because we had to move away from the grill to use it. But other innovations quickly followed, and several months later we could take orders from additional cars.

In-N-Out Burger began when two slightly acquainted men quit their jobs, combined their assets, and barely managed to erect a building on an isolated rural lot to start a business that neither knew how to do. As I see it, the DNA of In-N-Out is made up of small improvements and a simple menu where quality, the customer, friendliness, and cleanliness have always been important.

After Harry's passing, the management of In-N-Out moved to Rich, Guy, and Esther. Now Lynsi, Guy's daughter, is president and owner of the company, and I can tell you with complete confidence that Harry would be stunned and pleasantly surprised by what his sons and granddaughter have done.

When I joined the company there was no such thing as two-way speakers or a drive-thru! These In-N-Out concepts would be replicated nationwide and eventually in other places worldwide! I feel fortunate to have been an early part of it, all because I was blessed to have been in the right place at the right time and overheard a couple of fellows talking about a hamburger stand with a job opening.

Introduction

WHEN YOU'RE HUNGRY

MAYBE YOU LIVE IN CALIFORNIA OR YOU'VE FLOWN IN FOR VACATION or business. Your plane's just landed, and now you're famished. Where might you go? You want quality you can taste.

Or maybe you're somewhere in Oregon or Nevada and it's lunchtime. Or it's dinnertime in Colorado or Utah. Could be you're searching for the perfect afternoon snack or late-night meal in Arizona or Texas.

If you're anywhere close to one of the nearly four hundred locations in seven states and 280 cities, you know exactly where you're headed. Your mouth is watering even before you see the cheerful white-and-red restaurant. There's its famed yellow boomerang arrow sign. The arrow points to pride.

You spot two impossibly crossed palm trees growing outside the building. There's a fun story behind them, but only a few people know it. (Don't worry, I'll tell you soon.) You park your car or nose into the drive-thru.

You won't find a cluttered menu in this hamburger restaurant. No chicken fingers or French toast. You know deep down that when a restaurant specializes in only a few items—and has been around for seventy-five years—they've mastered the soul of their craft. Here's what you'll find:

Hamburger.

Cheeseburger.

Double-Double.

French fries.

Beverages. Shakes.

It's that easy. The straightforward menu feels nostalgic. Comforting. It reminds you of a simpler way of life. You're not blitzed with too many choices. You can be certain the menu has changed little since this restaurant first opened more than seven decades ago. Besides, you already know what you're going to order. Your favorite.

Maybe it's Combo Number 1. *Oh yeah*. Double-Double. Fries. Soda. Two 100 percent American beef patties with American cheese, hand-leafed lettuce, tomato, spread, with or without onions, stacked high on a freshly baked bun. Yum.

But you may have heard rumors of an entire secret menu that's not shown in the store or the drive-thru. It's actually not so secret, because you can find most of it on the restaurant's website. (For the rest, you just need to keep your ear to the ground.) Have you ever tried your burger Animal Style? Amazing! Have you ever ordered a Flying Dutchman? Do you know where its name came from? (Hint: Keep reading—I'll tell you soon.)

Whatever you order, you know that from your first bite of burger to your last French fry, quality is the most important ingredient here. None of the food you'll get at this iconic eatery is frozen, prepackaged, put under a heat lamp, or microwaved. Everything is made the old-fashioned way. Fresh. Hot. Delicious. That's what a hamburger's all about.

Maybe you'll pick up a cool T-shirt while you're here. Go ahead—ask for a paper hat. The friendly associate working behind the counter will smile and hand you one for free. Take a quick peek underneath your cup: you'll see a Bible verse. This company practices what it preaches.

All customers are treated with respect. All employees are called *associates*, and all of them are paid well—far above industry norms. They receive benefits and vacation days. They can participate in profit-sharing and retirement plans. Full-time associates receive health insurance. It's a fun, fast-paced place to work where a smile is part of the uniform.

The company gives back to its communities too. Through its namesake foundation it helps abused and neglected children. Through its newest foundation it opens paths to freedom to those who are enslaved by any person or substance. This company feeds the homeless. It cares for foster kids. It provides disaster relief assistance and supports firefighters.

And this company has an air of cool. It holds classic car shows, rock concerts, basketball tournaments, company picnics, and more. Colorful artwork is part of their culture. You can even find the associates at drag races.

That's just a quick glimpse of the place where so many of you love to eat. You know the name. You know exactly where to go.

In-N-Out Burger.

A Legacy in the Making

Hi, I'm Lynsi. I'm the granddaughter of our company's founders, Harry and Esther Snyder, and my heart is completely connected to In-N-Out Burger. In the pages ahead you'll hear more of our company's story. I want to tell you about who we are, why we do what we do, and what sets us apart. We're a fiercely independent family business, and we intensely cherish our history and legacy—and you.

My grandparents started In-N-Out Burger in 1948 as a tiny hamburger stand in Baldwin Park, California. My grandfather flipped burgers at the very first grill in a tiny store that was barely 100 square feet. Each day before dawn he visited nearby meat and produce markets to pick out fresh ingredients for the food that he prepared by hand. My grandmother prepped food and diligently handled all the bookkeeping and finances. Everybody loved her, and I grew up witnessing my grandmother's faith, which sustained her through both good and hard times.

Seventy-five years later, In-N-Out Burger is an internationally recognized company employing more than thirty-eight thousand associates. We're one of America's most respected restaurant chains. A-list celebrities post selfies taken in front of our stores. Award-winning chefs have dubbed us their favorite restaurant. When we've opened stores in new locations, our incredibly loyal customers have lined up around the block, either on foot or in their cars, sometimes even requiring police officers to direct traffic.

We do this all with little advertising. You'll hear a few radio commercials here and there. Every so often you'll watch a TV commercial featuring the jingle "In-N-Out, In-N-Out. That's What a Hamburger's All About." Mostly we rely on word of mouth.

We don't pull people in by offering gimmicky plastic toys. There's no breakfast items, chicken strips, or salad bars. We didn't strategize our way to success by using any blockbuster movie tie-ins (except one, to an old 1963 comedy starring Spencer Tracy). In many ways it seems we practice the antithesis of what many of today's successful companies do. By design, we have no outside investors and no plans to franchise. If we became a publicly traded company, we could undoubtedly earn more money. But that's not one of our highest goals. Some things in life and business are more important than lining our pockets. We're not trying to show up in every city in America, or all over the globe.

We like to keep things simple. We are laser-focused on quality, and we place a huge value on you as the customer. Our loftiest goal is to consistently offer you the best. Toward that aim, each store is strategically located within driving distance of an In-N-Out warehouse. Our meat department accepts only the highest quality front quarter beef chucks. Our own butchers carve out the highest quality beef, then patty our burgers. We maintain exacting standards so you receive the freshest and best food served quickly, for a good value, and in a friendly way. It's what you expect. It's what you deserve.

But our accomplishments didn't all come smoothly. Sometimes people say, "Hey Lynsi, you have success, you have money. You must have it easy."

Nope. Money doesn't buy happiness. And nobody's life is problem-free. We're real people who have made our share of mistakes, and our company has been hit by hard times—even tragedy. Our road has been far from easy. But we learn from our mistakes, from struggles and challenges. In this book I won't shy away from telling the difficult stories, too, because by telling them we can all be pointed toward hope. Hard times don't need to define us. There's a lot of freedom found in honesty. Together, when we share our stories, we can help each other overcome our challenges and thrive.

To really capture the spirit of the last seventy-five years, I called on my In-N-Out family, some of whom were there in the early years. Many of our associates have worked for In-N-Out for decades—twenty, thirty, even forty years. We even have seven associates who have hit the fifty-year mark.* That speaks volumes. Dozens of associates and vendors, past and present, contributed their stories to help create this book.

I also asked our official In-N-Out historian, Tom Moon, for his insight. With his help I dug down deep into the archives of our family business— the data, maps, photographs, and handwritten notes, plus audio and visual recordings of our founders. We'll share with you the best of the best of those.

And of course, I made sure to include personal memories and reflections as a Snyder family representative. I'm Harry and Esther's only grandchild, and I'm honored to call them family.

Piecing the whole story together has been a joyful adventure. I've been so blessed as I've heard from the many people who've made and are still making In-N-Out such a remarkable place.

A Different Kind of Company

I want to tell you this right up front. For me, the absolute most important aspect of our business is one you don't hear much about in business anymore.

God.

---

* The seven fifty-year associates are Chuck Papez, Bob Lang Sr., Joe Gee, Ben Ruley, Ray Maldonado, Wendell Ansnes, and Gary Murphy. Congratulations, all!

The faith embedded in In-N-Out Burger began with my grandmother. Eventually it found its way to my grandfather, then extended to my father and my uncle. And I've been a believer as long as I can remember. Our faith, put in its simplest terms, is about following the person, ministry, and teachings of Jesus Christ and knowing he is the Son of God.

Of course, at In-N-Out we don't only employ people who think or believe the way I do. All are welcome through our doors—to work or to eat—and I never try to force my faith on anyone. But I'm not shy about it either. It's incredibly important. I believe we need more good values, love, and compassion in this world today—not less. My faith has certainly helped me. By God's grace, I'm still alive today. By his power I strive to do some good in this world both individually and through our company. God is the glue that holds In-N-Out Burger together, and I never forget who's ultimately responsible for our success.

Faith also informs our two foundations that I mentioned earlier. A core mission of In-N-Out Burger is assisting our communities—helping make them better, stronger, and safer places to live.

Our namesake, the In-N-Out Burger Foundation, was established in the 1980s by my uncle, grandma, and mom to help fight and prevent child abuse—a cause near and dear to their hearts, as you'll soon read more about. Recently we've extended that mission to include caring for children aging out of the foster-care system.

Then in 2016, my husband, Sean, and I formed a second foundation, Slave 2 Nothing. This organization helps fight substance abuse addiction and works to end human trafficking, one of the most devastating problems plaguing our world today.

Both foundations are doing important work, helping people, literally saving lives—and we invite you to join us on this mission. We believe in these causes so strongly that we're donating every dollar of our proceeds from this book to our two foundations. We want to see people set free with hope and love in their future. You can feel good knowing you're helping these important causes.

By the end of this book, I hope you'll have a more complete picture of our company and a better understanding of what we do. If you're a fan of In-N-Out, you'll enjoy hearing behind-the-scenes stories about our history and culture. This is a story about the American dream in action, and wherever you're coming from, I know you'll find something to bring you hope, inspiration, and fun. If you're an entrepreneur or business leader interested in knowing more about running a successful privately owned company, you'll be encouraged to see that while it can be difficult, it is possible. If you're an individual struggling with personal challenges right now, you'll be inspired to see how ordinary people can learn, grow wiser, and overcome. If you are a leader who is feeling the strain, you'll realize it's the people and God who make you strong and able to weather the storm better. Being generous and loving others brings you joy through tough times. It's all part of the In-N-Out story.

Every day, we work hard at In-N-Out Burger to turn the freshest, highest quality ingredients into the iconic burgers that have created so much loyalty. We also work hard to turn our communities into places of compassion. We cherish our history, and I've invested my heart into this company and this book. I hope you enjoy reading it.

God bless you.

Lynsi Snyder

president and owner of In-N-Out Burger
Baldwin Park, California
May 2023

Chapter One

A LEGACY OF EXCELLENCE

Trust in the Lord with all your heart
And do not lean on your own understanding.
In all your ways acknowledge Him,
And He will make your paths straight.

Proverbs 3:5–6 NASB

TWENTY-THREE YEARS AGO I MADE A PROMISE TO MYSELF THAT I'D BE here: on the racetrack. And today I'm back.

I'm sitting tight in my Top Sportsman 1969 Chevelle, completely focused on the mechanics of what I must do. I run through my mental checklist and press the fuel, ignition, and starter. The huge engine rumbles and makes my heart happy.

It's go time.

I pull out onto the track, look toward the end of the dragstrip, and see the In-N-Out Burger logo atop the LED board. The arrow points to pride and reminds me of why I'm here today. Part of the legacy I've been given is a consistent drive toward excellence.

Putting my car in second gear to do a really big burnout, I can't help but smile as smoke billows from my tires. My crew backs me up to line up, and I flip the switch for race mode.

Here I am: forty years old, a mom of four, the president and owner of a successful company, and I have such a low resting heart rate it's almost a miracle. Had I joined the army at eighteen instead of getting married, I could have been a sniper. But I don't want a sense of calm in this moment. When I'm behind the wheel of a 1,600-horsepower car, I don't want to feel mellow. I want to feel amped for a quick reaction time.

I start to pull up to my stage. My opponent has been waiting, and as I break the beam, the 0.5-second lights are triggered. Instantly my foot goes on the brake, my thumb goes to the steering wheel for the transbrake button, and my right foot floors the accelerator.

I launch my Chevelle forward like a rocket, and I'm going three and a half Gs. I fight the steering wheel in small increments. Every millisecond counts. The end of the track approaches and I push my car to its limits, squeezing out every last bit of speed. I fly over the finish line and deploy my parachutes. I feel a tug on my chest, but as the car slows, I'm no longer thinking about the race. My mind instantly flashes to my dad. I know he would be so proud.

I see my time for the quarter mile: 6.7 seconds at 206 miles per hour.

A great number.

My eyes grow misty. I'm not a big crier, but I just wish my dad was here to see it all happen at the track that now bears our family company name—the In-N-Out Burger Pomona Dragstrip. The same place where we celebrated his life after his passing.

I'm instantly transported back to the day in December 1999 when I said my final goodbye to him. I was only seventeen. It was exactly the type of celebratory event that my dad would have wanted—one that reflected the very essence of his fun-loving personality. I remember walking around the track and seeing his favorite cars, including the '69 Blue Dart that I would one day race (though I didn't know it at the time). The smell of the grilled onions from the In-N-Out Cookout Truck filled the air that day as well as the sounds of some of the greatest rock 'n' roll tunes of the last few decades. I felt my dad's spirit. When I heard David Bowie's "Magic Dance" from *Labyrinth*—our favorite movie to watch together—blasting through the speakers, the tears began to flow. I made my way out to the lanes, looked down, and promised, "I'll be back"—to honor his memory and to celebrate the future of the company he dedicated so much of himself to.

Excellence Runs Through It

Fast cars and great food. They just go well together, and they're both a big part of the In-N-Out Burger legacy. My tears at the finish line of the Pomona race twenty-three years after my dad's celebration of life are because I'm thinking about the legacy I was handed from my father, my uncle, and my grandparents, a legacy I want to help shape and refine.

Let me explain this idea from its roots. My dad's heart was a big blown engine, and his blood was filled with adrenaline and racing fuel. To me, he was the coolest guy in the world. He rode motorcycles, and he enjoyed drag racing his whole life. I started racing when I was eighteen, but he died before he could see me race.

My dad is a big reason why I race today. I want to be connected to the sport he loved so much. I have great memories of being at the track as a kid, and every second was special.

Even though he's not physically with me at today's race, I'm surrounded by family. My mom is here, and I know that watching me race down the track at lightning speed scares her. But she trusted my dad's racing ability, and she knows that same instinct and skill are within me. She isn't the only one cheering me on today from the stands. I'm surrounded by my In-N-Out family, many of whom knew my dad and have supported and encouraged me.

I'm so grateful for this gift. Dad wasn't perfect, just like I'm not perfect. But he did so many things right. I want In-N-Out Burger to be the best company ever. I want to make my family proud.

It's not easy. I rely on my faith and those around me to help, including my mom and my two sisters, Teri and Traci. Though my sisters were already teenagers when I was born, they've had a huge influence on my life. Today, being a mom of four, I love and appreciate the relationship I have with my sisters, their five grown children (who are actually closer in age to me than my sisters are), and their grandchildren. Even more, I'm so grateful for what wonderful aunts they are to my kids, never hesitating to take on "aunt duties" when we need an extra hand.

With sisters, Traci and Teri, and mother, Lynda.

I have a lot on my plate, and it feels like I constantly need to work on scheduling. Work has never been busier, but I'm confident my priorities are in a good place now. I'm able to pick up each of my four children from school at least one day a week. I'm home before dinner, often making a meal for my family. I go on planned dates, separately, with my husband and kids—at least every other week with each person. I have a good rhythm. And In-N-Out Burger is going better than ever.

In my personal life and in my professional life, I want to be all I can be for my family, my company, my ministry, and my customers. Good decisions help excellence run through everything we do.

No Shortcuts to Greatness

What's true for families is also true for businesses. To make sure we grow and thrive at In-N-Out Burger, we identify what is best for our In-N-Out family and customer. We work hard to intentionally teach and train our people about what those best things are—practices that go beyond the norm. As we chart our company's course, we make sure everyone has what they need to get where they want to go. What might this course of excellence look like at In-N-Out Burger? Let me offer one example.

People ask me what it takes to lead our strong company. You definitely need to offer a quality product that's consistent and deliver that product to customers in a quick, friendly way. But I'd say if you truly want a company to be all it can be, start by treating your employees right. (I personally call them family. Although I've lost my family on my dad's side, they left me with thousands of people who I love and love to love.)

Companies are sometimes known for chewing through employees and spitting them out. For employees, it's become trendy to jump companies, never declaring loyalty, always on the hunt for a better position. At In-N-Out Burger we try to reverse those patterns.

It's not easy to get a job at the higher levels at In-N-Out. Every associate who works in or leads our stores was hired at the entry level, then worked their way up. We deliberately champion a slow-growth philosophy. Long ago we decided to grow only as fast as we can develop quality leaders. We don't grow to grow. With quality leaders in place, we can continue to ensure our high standards and grow at a calculated pace.

Lynsi Snyder's Three Favorite Orders at In-N-Out

1. If I'm super hungry I order double meat, extra spread, chopped chilies, and pickles only—with fries.
2. If I have a show coming up, I order double meat, mustard, pickles, and chilies—protein style.
3. If I'm detoxing, I order two mustard-fried patties.

Strategically, that means that every operations leader has done the exact jobs as the associates they're leading. They understand each one of those tasks, hands on, all the way up the line. They earned their way into their roles. Our culture of excellence includes an attitude of humility and hard work, just like my dad taught me.

Today our average store manager has been with the company for more than fifteen years. They're committed to In-N-Out, and we reward that commitment. Yes, we pay well. Currently, our average store manager earns more than $180,000 per year, which includes sharing in their store's profits. Offering the highest wages in the industry is one way we attract the best people to care for our customers, a practice that begins at entry level. Then we offer raises quickly after an associate masters different positions.

It doesn't matter if you've worked in a restaurant before. Everybody at In-N-Out starts the same way. First we teach you how to interact with our customers the In-N-Out way at the front counter or drive-thru windows—with a smile and genuine friendliness. You then learn how to take a customer's order accurately. Along the way you'll learn to prepare our fresh produce: coring and slicing tomatoes, peeling and dicing potatoes, hand-leafing lettuce, and peeling, slicing, and chopping onion. You'll go on to learn how to host in our dining room. When you master these areas you'll earn your first raise, often about a month after being hired. It's all part of the In-N-Out legacy: do it right and do it with a smile.

Next you'll work in the drive-thru operation, then learn to cook and serve quality French fries. Each role comes with its own pay raise and job level. Then you've got to master the salad table (also called the "board" because the stainless countertop where burgers are dressed and wrapped was a wooden board in the early days). The salad table requires quick thinking and quick hands, which means a lot of practice.

After all this experience you're ready to be trusted with our burgers, the most important piece of our menu. You're ready to learn the grill. The burger detail is considered a high privilege at In-N-Out, and it comes with the biggest pay bump yet.

It's funny, sometimes people will talk about "going to flip burgers," like that's a job they'll do if everything else doesn't work out. Maybe at other restaurants a person can get hired and be flipping burgers the next day. But at In-N-Out flipping burgers is a really big achievement. When you flip burgers at In-N-Out, you're in the captain's chair. You're steering the ship. Our burgers are our golden egg, our pride and joy. That's why nobody gets to flip burgers at In-N-Out until they've mastered the other levels. It's no small task to get every single burger perfect. Mastering all associate levels can be a one- or two-year process for a dedicated associate (although they may progress at a pace of their choosing).

We've gone all out to make sure that if our associates want to make intentional decisions to grow, we will support them. In fact we put together a framework to guide them however far they want to go. We have a management program for associates who show leadership potential and an aptitude for operating the business. Steps include more extensive in-store training, passing an evaluation week, and classroom work at In-N-Out University, which I'll tell you more about later.

Our store managers treat the business as if it's their own. We empower them to have an owner's perspective. These leaders have the most direct impact on the experience of our customers through the quality, friendliness, and cleanliness standards that they uphold. It's a big job, an important job, and I believe our team of store managers is the best in the world.

Beyond the stores we have fifty-five divisional managers who oversee divisions of six to eight stores, and nine regional managers who each oversee six to seven divisions. Our DMs and RMs are seasoned veterans of In-N-Out Burger—proven high-level leaders with track records of maintaining and growing the In-N-Out culture of seven decades.

Here's my point. We want to build success into every person who works for our company. We want people to grow with us. We want to add value to their lives while they are leading others. We want them to learn how to make good or even extraordinary decisions right from the start, then stay with our company for the long-term. That experience translates to our customers' experience. That's the legacy of our family life down through the years.

Throughout its history In-N-Out has been blessed with dedicated associates who have made it the strong company it is today.

When we develop great associates, this ensures customers are treated well every single time they come into a store. And customers are the reason we exist.

A Legacy of Excellence

Personally, to unlock this legacy of excellence and learn from it and then build on it, I've needed to look back and uncover the reasons my father, uncle, and grandparents made certain moves. When they succeeded in their roles, they had a strong personal drive and a strong team committed and dedicated to them. When they made mistakes or did things an unconventional way, there were always reasons.

For example, my father was vice president, then chairman of the board for several years (I'll tell you more about his journey later). He rose to the challenge and did a great job, continuing to grow In-N-Out Burger from its humble origins into a brand that's trusted and respected worldwide. He

cared deeply about In-N-Out but he definitely had a different way of showing his care than my Uncle Rich, who ran the company before him. My
dad, he hated suits. He was most comfortable in blue jeans, fatigues, shorts,
or even sweats and a T-shirt. I'm with him on that one. I have my own style
that usually means comfort.

My dad enjoyed being dressed casually not only because it fit his personality but also because he experienced so much physical pain. When he
was twenty-six, Dad was racing motorcycles in the desert with a friend and
flew over a cliff. His motorcycle landed on top of him, crushing his arm
and twisting his back. Doctors fused his arm and shoulder back together
the best they could. They reassembled his body with plates and screws. But
Dad never healed completely.

After his accident, he couldn't sit for long meetings. In his later twen-
ties, Dad oversaw In-N-Out's warehouse and meat processing, which suited
him better than sitting at a desk all day. He could manage his pain better,
enough even to continue racing cars and working on them in his spare time.
But he was never a conventional leader.

By the time I was born in 1982, In-N-Out Burger had been around for
more than thirty-four years and had become a staple of Southern California
life. As a young child I didn't know that my grandparents had started the
company. I didn't know that my uncle Rich was president of the company
and my dad was vice president. The themes and patterns of In-N-Out were
already being woven into the fabric of my life.

I have a memory of when we were all at our house. I'm four, maybe five.
Dad is grilling some mouthwatering hamburger patties and steaks over
charcoal. It's a summer evening, and the smoky smell of barbecue is wafting
up from our place, spreading all over the neighborhood. All this goodness
is emerging from our backyard.

"Samps!" Dad calls.

"Samps" means samples. It's a call for me to come and test a bite. He's aiming for perfection. He's wanting to achieve excellence, even in grilling dinner for his family. (Dad loved abbreviating words. Years later, I still use his coined word "samps" and many others.)

I run up to my dad and he hands me a taste. The bite is delicious. I chew it with a contented sigh, and I look at Dad. I look at him hard. He nods at me and grins. I sense, even as a child, that it's his way of letting me know I'm everything to him. Throughout my childhood, he lets me know in many small ways that he's confident my future's bright, even though I'll make mistakes along the way.

"You know, Lynsi," he said to me later, and many times in my young years, "you can do anything you put your mind to."

That's the legacy I'm part of.

A legacy of excellence, a legacy of belief. This line of love and support and strength and hope runs all through my family, and I feel the responsibility to continue that same positive outlook today for my own children, for our company. For you.

At work I make decisions every day by asking this question: "What would my family think?" I'm enormously proud of my family, our history, and our people at In-N-Out. I love our customers and I want what's best for their lives. Latching hold of legacy helps a person live a better life. It reminds us that time is short, and we all need to make the most of every day.

So to get the full story of In-N-Out Burger, let's go back to the beginning. It all started with a hardworking husband-and-wife team, a problem solver and his compassionate partner: Harry and Esther Snyder. And it began with one good idea—maybe even a great one.

ATV riding with her father, Guy Snyder, on his, Gram's, and Harry's land in Covina.

Chapter Two

ONE SMALL HAMBURGER STAND

Whether you eat or drink or whatever
you do, do it all for the glory of God.

1 CORINTHIANS 10:31 NIV

HE WAS A POWERHOUSE OF A MAN PACKED INTO A TIGHT, MUSCLED frame: five feet eight-and-a-half inches tall, 172 pounds. He had a ruddy complexion, brown eyes, and brown hair.[1] He could be tough and exacting, and he believed in his own motto: "Keep it real simple. Do one thing and do it the best you can."

My knowledge of my grandfather, Harry Snyder, is pieced together from family stories, old photographs, and grainy video footage. He died six years before I was born, and although my grandmother didn't speak of him much when I was little, she talked about him often toward the end of her life. Taking my hand in hers, she whispered stories of how he'd poured his heart and soul into In-N-Out Burger. Whether he built the company for his family or raised his family to run the company is a question I wonder about to this day. He had a rough childhood and came from little. I believe he had dreams to make things better for his family. As a child I felt fiercely loved and protected by the adults in my life, and when my dad told me, "Your grandfather would've loved you," I believed it.

My grandfather was extremely focused and a stickler for detail. Born to

Dutch immigrants in Vancouver, British Columbia, on September 9, 1913, Harry was only a toddler when his family crossed the border to Seattle, Washington, seeking better work opportunities. For Harry and his two older sisters, childhood was no picnic. Money was always tight. Their father, Henrick, painted houses and apartments and never stayed with one job for long. Harry's mother, Mary, cleaned houses to help make ends meet. Apparently Henrick could be a difficult man. Once he landed in jail after an argument with a landlord. He didn't stay behind bars for long, as the story goes. But he was a challenging person to the end, sometimes taking out his hard emotions on his wife and kids.

When Harry was still a boy, his family left the Pacific Northwest and moved to California, where young Harry delivered newspapers, sold sandwiches for a grocery store, and worked odd jobs. He graduated from Venice High School in 1931, at the height of the Great Depression, and attended college for one semester before dropping out due to a lack of funds. He found work with the railroad, then enlisted in the army on November 23, 1942, as a private. Harry was twenty-nine years old. A perforated eardrum kept him from being deployed overseas with the infantry, but he served stateside during World War II in the army's records department, mostly as a clerk.

My grandmother, Esther Lavelle Johnson, was equally hardworking but a gentler soul. She was born in Illinois on January 7, 1920, where her father mined coal. In a family of eight children—seven girls and one boy—Esther was fourth oldest. Like Harry, she grew up with little money. When she was fourteen, her town's hardscrabble coal mine closed, and her dad lost his job. The family managed to scrape together enough cash to stay put, keep eating, and not lose hope. An aunt helped Esther attend Greenville College for two years, after which she taught school. When war broke out, she enlisted in the newly formed WAVES Program (Women Accepted for Voluntary Emergency Services)—an oddity for the nation, not to mention her family. After basic training Esther assisted surgical nurses for the navy in a burn ward in San Diego. What compassion and courage she must've shown! By the time the war ended, she was a pharmacist's mate first class.

My grandmother was petite, maybe eight inches shorter than my grandfather—five foot even, or five foot one. She had dark brown hair that she curled daily and a ready, infectious smile. I've seen pictures that show her as a very beautiful young woman. After the war she didn't return to Illinois and enrolled in Seattle Pacific University in Washington State, where she earned a bachelor's degree in zoology. Soon she became the day manager of the commissary at Fort Lawton, overlooking the gray-blue waters of Puget Sound, where—when she was twenty-seven—she met the man who would become my grandfather.

Harry had returned to Seattle after the war ended. He was thirty-four in 1947 and selling boxed lunches at the shipyards when he met Esther. Whenever a fleet came in, he'd make as many as fifteen hundred sandwiches, developing skills he'd use just a couple of years later. One day he was delivering sandwiches to the commissary—"Boxes and boxes of sandwiches," my grandmother shared later. They met, dated, and fell in love. It was the makings of a good team. My grandmother was highly intelligent and resourceful. My grandfather was responsible, innovative, and optimistic. In 1948 they married.

Together they planned to build a better life than the ones they'd been born into. Their ticket to success would be one small hamburger stand.

Humble Roots

In the years immediately following World War II, optimism flourished in the United States. It was an era for getting on with life, marrying your sweetheart, buying a home, and having children. Scores of newly married American vets were pursuing the American dream just like Harry and Esther. In 1948, the same year they married, my grandparents decided to make another radical change. Harry was an entrepreneur at heart, and he saw that the American economy was now booming. He dreamed up an idea for a new kind of business.

Americans were growing increasingly mobile. Gas was cheap, and

Americans loved their new Chevys, Chryslers, and Fords. Harry imagined creating a new restaurant that would offer fast but quality meals for people on the go. In Olympia, just south of Seattle, he'd seen a restaurant where cars drove right up to a window to order. The drivers didn't even turn off their engines. They received their food, paid, and just kept going. Harry believed he could be successful with a similar restaurant where customers could go "in and out" that quickly. He already had the knowledge and experience of working in the food services industry. But he dreamed of a bigger location than Olympia, somewhere on the West Coast. He wondered: Where would it make the most sense to begin a new business? What city?

They decided on Los Angeles. He and Esther packed their bags and moved to Southern California. You might think dropping everything to move a thousand miles south to start a new restaurant would worry the young bride. "Not for one minute," my grandmother told me. "If you were ever around Harry for any length of time, you just knew he would be successful at whatever he put his mind to"—a notion similar to what my dad later shared with me.

Los Angeles attracted my grandparents for a number of reasons. First, my grandfather knew the area, having graduated from high school in Venice, a neighborhood on the west side. Second, California as a whole was rich in agriculture, and during the war the ship and airplane manufacturing industries had rapidly expanded. When the war ended, vets were relocating to Los Angeles in droves, spurred on by California's sunny climate and the promise of family-wage jobs. Los Angeles meant a large and growing population, with each worker having a dollar to spare. With my grandparents' drive, heart, dedication, and lots of elbow grease factored in, the City of Angels offered a prime location to begin a new business.

My grandfather wasn't as well-educated as my grandmother. But he had street smarts and was a problem solver. He had a stubbornness and wouldn't give up easily. If he put his mind to something, he worked to see it through to completion. He was constantly curious, always looking to make things better. And he believed the marketplace would reward good ideas.

First up, Harry needed an investor. A friend named Charlie Noddin had worked as a supervisor for Langendorf Bakery in Seattle, where he'd met Harry when selling him bread for his lunch business. At age fifty-two, Charlie was looking for a short-term investment to fund his retirement. Charlie liked Harry and could see he was a hard worker. They combined resources, coming up with $5,000 seed money. The Noddins moved south too.

It wasn't much money to go on, but Harry and Charlie both believed in the vision. So did their wives, Esther and Margaret. Harry began searching for a good location for a restaurant in the LA basin. Not much was available. He searched for some time before locating an available piece of property in Baldwin Park, almost twenty miles from downtown Los Angeles. It wasn't a perfect piece of commercial real estate by any means. But it was affordable, and Harry was looking toward the future.

These days, Baldwin Park is fully enmeshed in the metroplex of Los Angeles, but in 1948 it was mostly rural, dotted with dairies, walnut farms, and orange groves. Harry also saw a new trailer park and clusters of new small, stick-built "GI homes." That meant lots of young families and commuters. He could see that the downtown core was growing outward, creating suburbs and a car-dependent culture. Baldwin Park lay right in the path of opportunity.

They secured a small piece of property on the corner of Francisquito Avenue and Garvey, a main thoroughfare to cities east of Los Angeles. Harry sketched a simple ten-foot by ten-foot hamburger stand, and construction began. As the cement foundation was poured, neighbors tried to guess what business it might be. The building was so tiny, some wondered if it was set to be a service station.[*]

Once the spartan store was completed, the partners' modest start-up cash had dwindled to just $1,500—and there was still equipment to purchase and inventory to stock. Harry believed the most important part of the equation was the quality of the food, so he outfitted the small stand with a

---

[*] John Cassianni told us that he wondered if the stand would become a gas station. He was one of In-N-Out Burger's first customers. Later he became a longtime In-N-Out associate and store manager. John Cassianni, interview with In-N-Out researcher, 2022.

good used grill, two good used fryers, and a brand-name Coldspot refrigerator. The salad table for prepping orders was bought new, as was the kitchen sink. Later they would add a shed out back for storing potatoes, cases of bottled sodas, and a sealed steel cabinet for freshly made buns.

Harry wanted his menu to be simple: hamburgers, cheeseburgers, fries, drinks, and coffee. He and Esther planned to hand-patty the burgers themselves, then cook them on the grill and dress them to order on toasted buns. They'd offer perfectly prepared, fresh-cut fries as well as sodas. Both Pepsi and Coke would be offered (this was before the cola wars started in the 1970s) as well as root beer, 7UP, cream soda, orange and strawberry sodas, and a grape-flavored soda called Delaware Punch.

Finally they installed a sign. White letters on a red background proudly proclaimed

IN-N-OUT HAMBURGERS: NO DELAY

On October 22, 1948, at 4:15 p.m., Harry and Esther Snyder and their business partners, Charlie and Margaret Noddin, officially opened In-N-Out Hamburger, California's first drive-thru. That first chilly night they sold fifty-seven burgers. Hamburgers sold for 25 cents, cheeseburgers for 30 cents. A bottle of pop was a dime. Charlie may have felt nervous about his retirement plan, but Harry had faith. He believed that delicious burgers and fries, served fresh, fast, and with a smile, would win the day. By the end of the month, they'd sold two thousand burgers. (These days many of our stores easily sell that many burgers in one day!)

They were still short of an empire's worth. But they were well on their way.

Life in the Fishbowl

Hamburger stands of the late 1940s and 1950s often featured walk-up windows or carhops—waitstaff who shuttled burgers and fries to customers on roller skates. From the beginning In-N-Out was different, designed for drivers on the go. At In-N-Out, drivers pulled up to the window. They talked directly to the cook to place their orders, and they received their food in the comfort of their car.

My grandparents believed in transparency. They didn't want cooks hiding behind walls. The architecture of Store Number 1 was designed to be plain and functional. The tiny hamburger stand's most prominent feature was the oversized floor-to-ceiling windows. Customers could watch as their meal was prepared, their burgers grilled and dressed, and their fries freshly made. Through the enormous windows, every inch of the kitchen was visible, exactly as Harry had planned. He believed customers would enjoy seeing their food made with care. Transparency reinforced and broadcast In-N-Out's commitment to quality, freshness, and cleanliness. The great big windows are the origin of our in-house reference today to living life in the fishbowl.

While Harry found that customers appreciated the convenience of ordering from their cars, the system started awkwardly. As each order was being prepared, a cook had to stick his head out the window and ask the people in the next car what they'd like to order. Sometimes the cook would need to step outside to take an order.

Harry was innovative, always looking for ways to better serve the customer. He remembered seeing intercom systems used on military ships. Inspired, he wired together a two-way speaker system that allowed people to

fun FACT

A fun fact about putting together the intercom system: my grandfather was colorblind. He must have asked somebody the color of each wire to put the system together.

communicate directly with cooks. Harry used military-style speaker cones mounted on poles in the drive lanes.

In July 1949, Harry introduced the first drive-thru two-way speaker to the restaurant, posting a sign for drivers that read: "2-Way Speaker. For Your Convenience, Driver May Order Without Leaving Car." Today In-N-Out Burger has become the longest running family-owned drive-thru in history. We were also the first drive-thru in the world with a two-way speaker.

Three Fun Facts About In-N-Out Burger's First Drive-Thru Speakers

Before In-N-Out's founder, Harry Snyder, there was no such thing as a drive-thru speaker. Can you imagine?

1. **Hello? Is anybody there?** The idea of a drive-thru speaker was so new in 1949 that Harry had to introduce his customers to it and explain how to use it, or else they might get out of their car and start messing with the switches. That's why he posted a sign in red letters that read:

> **TWO-WAY Speaker:**
>
> **For Your Convenience,**
>
> **Driver May Order**
>
> **WITHOUT LEAVING CAR.**

2. **You had to know your cars.** The first speaker box was very simple and basically consisted of just a toggle switch, because there was only a single lane with one speaker to control. When the two-lane stores were built, Harry added a second speaker to each lane for a total of four speakers. For many years the speaker box design had all four speakers on at the same time. In those days associates greeted the car by type, calling out, "Hi, in the gray '48 Chevy, how are you tonight?" The mention of the make and model of the car let the customer know it was their turn.

3. **They might just get stolen.** From the 1950s to the 1970s, the lane speakers were usually unwired and dismounted at closing time so they wouldn't get stolen. (They made popular car accessories for both car stereos and horns.) The speakers were carefully stored in an empty crate. Harry was always very particular about the way the wires were wrapped during storage for two reasons: (1) if the wires were damaged, the speakers wouldn't work, and that would be very bad for business, and (2) Harry was colorblind, and if the wires weren't wrapped to his specifications, he had a hard time reinstalling the speakers the next morning.

Dressing professionally was important to Harry. He had proudly served the country in a military uniform, and for him wearing a uniform at In-N-Out meant showing respect for customers. Every day he wore a clean white shirt, white pants, a white apron secured with a safety pin, black shoes and belt, and a clean, white paper cap. Day after day, his In-N-Out uniform never varied.

When my grandparents first hired staff, they referred to employees as "helpers." In return, helpers called my grandfather "Harry." Both my grandparents wanted this to be a first-name company, but even so most called my grandmother "Mrs. Snyder" out of respect. Early photographs show helpers dressed exactly like Harry. Customers wouldn't see any difference between the owner and the helpers. What mattered was that the customers enjoyed a delicious meal, prepared perfectly.

Harry was particular about quality. Early each morning he drove to the Golden State Meat Company to make sure the butchers gave him the best cuts of meat. Harry would personally select the front quarter chucks, then he would stand and watch as the butchers deboned and ground the beef for him. The front quarter chuck was an expensive cut of meat, but Harry was willing to spend more to get the highest quality available. He would then bring the ground beef back to Store Number 1, where it was shaped into patties. (This went on until 1963, when we hired our first butcher, Martin Edwards. Today we hire and train our own butchers, who take great pride in helping us serve the burgers In-N-Out customers love.) Harry was so meticulous that all the butchers began referring to him as "Hamburger Harry." The man called "Hamburger Harry" never accepted anything less than his standard.

As In-N-Out began to grow, so did the city of Baldwin Park. By 1949, plans were being made for the expansion of the Interstate 10 freeway east from Los Angeles. With those plans came growth—and competition.

Across the street a new building was going up. One afternoon a regular customer of Harry's told him that the building was going to be a new steak house and that the owner had boasted he would run Harry out of business soon. "It really shook him up," Tom Evans, Harry's first helper, remembered.

Early the next morning, Harry made his usual visit to Golden State Meat. As always, he hand-selected the chucks he wanted, then he watched the butchers debone and grind the meat. But that day Harry noticed the butchers weren't following their normal routine. While the work they did for Harry was exactly as normal, they were setting aside their lower-quality beef in a separate pile. It grew larger by the minute.

"Who are those cuts for?" Harry asked.

"Know that new steak restaurant near you?" a butcher said. "For them."

Harry grinned. Back at the store he told Tom, "We're going to be fine. That steak house is in trouble but the owner doesn't even know it yet. People will try out a new restaurant once, but they will only come back for quality."

Within a year the steak house went out of business. Seventy-five years later, In-N-Out is still going strong.

Relentless

Harry and Esther both worked hard. Behind the scenes, Esther handled the books and paid all the invoices, mostly from home. She worked long hours too. Often she helped out in the store itself.

The ground chuck my grandfather hand-selected came back to the store in a heavy container called a lugger. (We still use this term today, although we have our own meat-patty production facilities now.) Harry and Esther then shaped each patty by hand. In videos (circa 1976) Harry recounted how they measured out each patty of meat using an ice-cream scoop. They used a manual press to shape each patty to perfection. It wasn't until October 2, 1963 (when we hired our first in-house butcher) that we acquired patty-making machines.

My grandparents selected the fresh produce and prepared it by hand, too, as we do to this day. Fresh iceberg lettuce was cored, washed, and separated at the board, then stored in one-gallon containers in the fridge. Tomatoes were washed, then cored with a knife and hand-sliced using an eight-inch, highly precise French knife—taking care to use the center cuts. (Two slices are used when not center cut.)

Onions were sliced using the same French knife. For the perfect balance of flavors, Harry insisted on same-sized—or close to it—slices of onions and tomatoes. When those tasks were complete, chopped onions were fried on the grill. Harry believed the aroma of cooked onions in the air would entice drivers to stop for a burger.

Harry dressed each burger with a special proprietary condiment similar to a Thousand Island dressing. He created the blend himself and referred to it simply as "spread." It was the perfect complement to the flawlessly grilled patty, melting cheese, and toasted bun. He kept the recipe under wraps, and it's always been made in-house. Our spread gives each In-N-Out burger an undeniably delicious, signature taste.

Onions—Call Them What You Will

If you were asked, "What type of onion does In-N-Out use?" and you answered "Bermuda," you would be partially correct but technically incorrect. The best terminology to use would be to reply, "We use US No. 1 jumbo yellow sweet onions."

In the early years of In-N-Out, Harry experimented with the produce items he chose because he was building a business from scratch. He tested different onions before deciding that the Bermuda was the onion of choice. Was it technically a Bermuda onion? Probably not, for three reasons:

1. Only onions grown on the island of Bermuda qualify as true Bermuda onions.
2. The true Bermuda is a spring onion and is not available year-round.
3. Since it was the original sweet onion and the only type available during the early twentieth century, the name "Bermuda" stuck as a generic name for all sweet onions.

The onions that Harry knew as Bermuda onions have a succulent, juicy texture and mild, sweet flavor without the harsh, spicy finish. This is what Harry wanted, so that the flavor of the onion would not overpower the flavor of the cooked meat patty and would complement the natural sugar of the caramelized toasted bun.

Harry offered three different options for preparing onions:

- **"With onions"**—Orders for "with onions" meant the slice of onion was placed on top of the meat or cheese patty to warm and soften the onion while the heat awakened the sugars and sweetened the onion flavor.
- **"Raw onions"**—Orders for "raw onions" called for the onion slice to be placed on the bottom bun, providing a crisper texture and a stronger onion flavor; again, the mild flavor of the Bermuda was chosen so that even a raw slice would not overpower the flavor balance.
- **"Grilled onions"**—Orders for "grilled onions" made use of the fact that the Bermuda onion is widely regarded as the best grilling onion. The natural sugars caramelize during the grilling process, producing a mild, sweet flavor.

These three options have evolved over the years to include other variations such as "chopped onion," "raw, chopped onion," and "whole-grilled onion."

But the reasoning behind the type of onions we purchase has never changed. When we say we use jumbo yellow sweet onions, it means we have chosen to use onions that would have met Harry's approval. These onions have the same characteristics as those Harry personally selected when he shopped for fresh produce at the LA produce markets.

Call them what you will, but rest assured that the onions we choose are of the highest quality and will be the perfect complement to the flavor of the cooked meat patty and the toasted bun.

Soon Harry and Esther hired more helpers, drilling into each new hire the uncompromising importance of quality. One day a guy walked in with some tomatoes he wanted to sell. Harry was out, but an industrious young helper named Bob Lang was on the floor. He bought them for two dollars and thought he'd made a good deal. When Harry returned, Bob said, "Hey, look at what I got."

Harry inspected the tomatoes, sniffed, and said, "I never want you to do that again."

The tomatoes weren't the best of the best.[2]

Customers loved the quality of In-N-Out. But Harry's pace began to catch up with him. Everything he and Esther owned was tied up in that little ten-by-ten hamburger stand. He averaged an eighty-hour workweek, and eighteen-hour days weren't uncommon. Many days, Harry rose early to shop for produce and meat. He'd return home and catch a catnap, then head to the store to open it by 11 a.m. He'd work in the store all day, head home for supper with Esther after the dinner rush, then return to close the store and clean the kitchen. He'd grab a couple hours of sleep, wake, and start the whole process over again.

Supper at home was a luxury he could indulge in since my grandparents' modest one-bedroom home was just across the street from the original In-N-Out. Harry, who'd lived in rentals all his life up until then, was proud to be a homeowner as well as a business owner. He worked hard for every penny he earned.

Still, the pace was relentless. How could they survive?

Chapter Three

A DRIVING PACE

The Lord is good, a refuge in times of trouble.
He cares for those who trust in him.

NAHUM 1:7 NIV

GROWTH AND HIRING DIDN'T HAPPEN OVERNIGHT. DURING IN-N-Out's first season, Harry cooked every day and led the charge to drive the business. As In-N-Out grew, Esther's bookkeeping and office responsibilities grew, too, and she had less time to spend in the store itself. But whenever possible she was at her husband's side doing whatever was needed—forming meat patties, slicing tomatoes, cutting French fries, opening, closing, cleaning up.

Charlie and Margaret Noddin worked just as hard, and at the start each couple worked seven days a week in rotations. For instance, Harry and Esther would work Sunday night and Monday day. Then Charlie and Margaret would take over for Monday night and Tuesday day. Keeping the restaurant open night and day kept In-N-Out afloat financially. They knew they needed to bring on employees soon, but Harry wanted to ensure his exacting standards were firm and would be replicated.

In-N-Out's first official hire came in March 1949: a lanky youth named Tom Evans. A hardworking, friendly, and industrious guy, he worked regular shifts then relieved the couples so they could each work six days instead of seven. Even so, it took time before Harry trusted Tom enough to leave him alone to run the store. When Harry finally went home to grab some rest, he kept an eye on the store from the window of his house. If Tom had a question or needed help, he could reach Harry through a direct phone line straight to the house.[1] If Harry saw the drive-thru line backing up, he'd hurry over and pitch in.

Years later my grandmother recalled how my grandfather prided himself on perfecting the methods for preparing and cooking In-N-Out burgers and fries. "Harry always said that you didn't give customers a burger unless it would be one that you would eat yourself," she said. "That burger had to be cooked right. You didn't want to make any mistakes. You wanted to give customers the correct order."[2]

How Things Were Done

Getting each order correct wasn't easy. From the start of In-N-Out in 1948 through the 1960s, order-taking was done entirely by memory, and it required quick and accurate math skills.

When a vehicle pulled up to the two-way speaker, the cook took the customer's burger order but didn't write it down. That took too much time. Patties were instantly sizzling on the grill. The driver then pulled up to the window, and the window associate confirmed the order and took the customer's fry and drink order. The window associate added up the price in his head, including tax. The next step was to "clear the car," which meant taking payment for the order. The window associate filled the customer's drink order and handed over the bottles, calling "All clear," confirming the customer had paid. Last, burgers and fries were handed to the customer, hot and fresh.

As the business grew, Harry noticed that a friendly young man named John Cassianni often ate at In-N-Out. John lived in the Baldwin Park neighborhood and loved the burgers. Harry knew it made sense to hire people who were already familiar with In-N-Out. One afternoon Harry asked if John needed a job. John shook his head with a grin and said he already had one, but he did need more hours. On the spot, Harry offered him a job with more hours plus higher pay. Minimum wage was sixty-five cents per hour, but Harry paid a dollar per hour, plus a free burger each shift.

"That sounds great," John said. "But I don't know how to cook."

"That's okay," Harry responded. "I'll teach you."[3]

Harry adopted the posture of a mentor. He saw each person he hired as someone he could help shape for good purposes. He didn't want people to stay in entry-level jobs forever. He expected them to learn from him what it took to start their own businesses or become managers in his stores someday. He appreciated loyalty, and he encouraged the best of the best of his trainees toward lifelong careers at In-N-Out.

While Harry's respect wasn't given easily, it could be earned. Equal opportunity laws were different in the 1940s and 1950s, and at the start Harry hired only young men. He feared that hiring women would prompt flirting, distracting helpers from their jobs. His mind stayed continually on business, and he often offered correction and feedback to the young men he hired. Still, he was generous and supportive.

For example, one day Harry noticed that young Chuck Papez's father picked him up at the end of each late-night shift. Harry told his new helper to give his father a break and buy himself a car. When Chuck lamented he didn't have enough money even for a down payment and no credit, Harry handed him a check for $600, enough to buy a good used car outright. It wasn't a gift. Chuck paid Esther a little each week until he'd met the terms of the agreement.* My grandparents' willingness to invest in people created a strong sense of mutual loyalty. Years passed, and Chuck became the first associate to reach fifty years with the company.

Harry taught each new helper to take pride in his appearance and workplace. Part of that pride meant maintaining a spotlessly clean store. Each night the kitchens were cleaned to exact standards, which extended to the

---

* The car loan story came from Bob Lang Sr., who was there the day Harry handed Chuck the check.

building and grounds. The parking lot was kept tidy. Trash was picked up and disposed of throughout each day. Though pavement for Store Number 1 wasn't in the budget, Harry laid fresh gravel in the driveway. The gravel was raked regularly to keep it free from weeds and debris. He lined the drive with rocks painted white to keep it all neat and tidy.

My grandfather wanted friendliness to be as much a part of the In-N-Out experience as the food, so he trained his helpers to think of each In-N-Out customer as a guest. Each guest must be greeted with a smile and a hearty welcome. It had to be genuine, too, so only the friendliest people were hired. Harry's legacy of hiring people with positive attitudes continues to this day.

Harry fostered a sense of teamwork. There wasn't much elbow room in that first tiny hamburger stand with the big windows. The original store was so small that only three people could work side by side comfortably. Everybody had to pitch in, help each other, and move in harmony. The close quarters fostered a team atmosphere that brought the helpers close together as friends.[4]

Word got out that Harry paid well and that working at In-N-Out was fast-paced, challenging, and exciting. A cheerful youth named Jack Ruley was soon hired. "It was a strong environment of friendship," recalls Jack. "When you got accepted with the guys, they gave you a nickname. You had

Guy Snyder giving his daughter, Lynsi, a kiss on the cheek.

a bond and enjoyed coming to work because you loved them and you loved what you did."[5]

The nicknaming tradition would continue for decades. Even I got one. My father had a way of imagining what animal a person reminded him of. When I was a child in the early 1980s, I liked hiding in tight places such as cabinets in our pantry and then waiting, usually so I could jump out and scare somebody or listen to conversations. One evening after I'd jumped out to scare him, Dad grinned and said, "You're just like a little red fox." I laughed out loud. He knew I had sharp discernment. (And these days I'm nocturnal with a pointy nose, short legs, and long torso.) The name fit. Today, I use Fox as my race name, and I have animal nicknames for a number of our divisional managers, regional managers, and executives—my family at home and "under the arrow."

One Store Becomes Many

While business was growing, Esther and Harry lived frugally. They had come of age during the Great Depression, and they worked hard for everything they owned, keeping track of every dollar earned and spent. I've seen detailed ledger entries showing how many shakes were sold at certain stores in the early 1950s.[†] This was before calculators were popularized, yet the entries in that ledger go out five decimal points, figured by hand. I'm fairly sure it's my grandmother's handwriting.

While they never scrimped on the best quality of food for customers, Harry and Esther pinched pennies rigorously. If a piece of equipment broke, Harry fixed it himself. Esther handed helpers their paychecks in recycled power company envelopes.[‡] Years later, even after the business had done very

---

† Most of the original ledgers are lost now. The one I saw came from the Pasadena store.
‡ Recycled-envelopes information came from Bob Lang Sr., part of the In-N-Out family since 1954. At the time of his retirement in 2013, Bob was working as a QFC evaluator, visiting all the stores to evaluate them for quality, friendliness, and cleanliness standards.

well, I have memories of helping my grandmother search for coupons from the Sunday newspaper before we'd head to the grocery store.

By living and spending modestly, my grandparents were able to invest In-N-Out profits back into the business. They handed out cash bonuses to their helpers at Christmas. Harry and Esther hated debt, and they decided that only when they'd saved up enough money to pay cash for land and construction would they build a new store. Harry insisted that they never owe anyone anything—and he dreamed of expansion. But he didn't rush or expand quickly. With an eye for sound strategy, he noticed that their drive-thru benefitted from proximity to heavily traveled roads, making it easy for commuters to pull in for a delicious meal with no delay. He began to hunt for similar locations for new stores.

In late 1949, In-N-Out Burger built and opened a second location at 823 South San Gabriel Boulevard. The design was similar to Store Number 1, with a single lane for drive-ups. But the new store also featured a window built for walk-up guests. Harry used an existing garage on the property for storage and as a location for daily prep.

My grandfather had poured so much into Store Number 1. With it setting the pace for quality, service, and friendliness, he wanted customers visiting Store Number 2 to receive the same—and he wanted that to be true whether he was present or not. Achieving that comfort level took time. He expected every helper to work hard and maintain a winning attitude. In exchange he paid well and taught them everything he knew.

In 1951, Harry built and opened two more stores. Store Number 3 was in Arcadia at 218 Huntington Boulevard, our first store with two drive-thru lanes. This third store marked more notable changes. Both Store Number 1 and Number 2 featured the iconic phrase "In-N-Out Hamburgers No Delay." Beginning with the third store, Harry shortened the company name to what it is today: In-N-Out Burger.

Store Number 3 presented new challenges. Since it featured two lanes and two speakers on each side of the store, plus an additional walk-up customer area, the cook had to be on top of his game. He needed to juggle six or more orders from the cars in the drive-thru lanes plus three or four from the walk-up window. Only the most qualified cooks with the sharpest memories worked at Store Number 3.

The original Store Number 4 was the only building where Harry didn't oversee construction. A competitor had built a restaurant on the location, but the business hadn't done well, so the competitor begged Harry to buy the building. Harry did some research and discovered that the odd-shaped property would soon be expropriated under eminent domain, the law that permits government to buy private property at a fair price for public use. The I-10 freeway was coming through in 1954, and this location would soon be swallowed up by the new road. Harry calculated that the fair market value paid by the government would be more than the price the competitor was asking. So when the government bought out Harry, he'd make a slight profit and could reinvest in a more valuable property later.

The building didn't have the signature slanted windows and drive-thru lane like the other stores. But it had a large walk-in box out back and the company's first mechanical potato peeler. Helpers from the other three stores drove over to peel their potatoes at the machine, which was positioned outside the back door. A benefit of sharing the peeler was that helpers started getting to know each other across all four stores.

In 1952, Store Number 5 opened in Pasadena at 2114 East Foothill Boulevard. This is our oldest store that's still standing today, and it's truly one of a kind. The store was quite a drive from Baldwin Park, since there were no freeways running by it at the time. Business in this location started out slow, so Harry tried a few unique sales techniques like installing a landscaped pond in a grassy area directly in front of the stand.

He served malts at Store Number 5, which added to its unique charm. He also started selling shakes made the old-fashioned way, a practice that eventually found its way to all In-N-Outs. The ice cream was scooped into a standard Sweetheart cup, milk and flavorings were added, then an Osterizer blender did the whipping. Harry liked to keep things simple, and only three milkshake flavors have ever been offered: strawberry, chocolate, and (my favorite) vanilla.

Harry built a small back room on the stand, and a few years later a second story was built on top of the back room. The top floor served as a storage area (or, as the story goes, a good place to sleep if you didn't want to drive home after a closing shift).

In 2002, the sign at Store Number 5 was designated a historic landmark by the city of Pasadena. As such, everything—from the sign's paint color to the bulbs in the arrow—must be preserved in the same state as the time of designation. The store has gone through extensive interior remodeling and upgrading over the years, but the exterior looks just as it did in the 1960s when the second story was built and a bright red corrugated metal roof wrap was added. It's a monument to a bygone era. To the best of our knowledge, Store Number 5 is the nation's oldest still-standing drive-thru. It's probably also the oldest still-standing double drive-thru in the world.

Harry and Esther at the Helm

At the end of 1952, Harry and Charlie amicably ended their partnership and divided up the stores. My grandparents took Stores Number 1, Number 4, and Number 5. Charlie and Margaret took Stores Number 2 and Number 3, and the soon-to-open Number 6 in Azusa. When Store Number 6 opened on Foothill Boulevard in February 1953, the fifty-fifty split was complete—or nearly. In the contract both parties agreed to keep

fun **FACT**

Store Number 1 still has the original phone number it opened with in 1948, and Store Number 4 has the phone number it reopened with in 1954.

The iconic In-N-Out arrow led to associates adopting
the saying, "The arrow points to pride."

the In-N-Out Burger name, but as part of the agreement, the name would change if either owner sold the business or gave it to a family member.

A couple of years later, Virginia and Bob Kleckner (Charlie's step-daughter and her husband) took over Charlie's business. The Noddins' son Donald ("Doc") was also instrumental in helping run the business. They changed their three stores' name to Bob's Beef Burgers. Bob Kleckner never expanded, and when they sold Store Number 6, it became Booth's Better Burgers under new owners, eventually becoming Volcano Burger before going out of business. The Noddin family sold Store Number 2 in 1979, and it no longer exists. The location was redeveloped in 1986. Store Number 3 is also gone today.

In 1954, the I-10 freeway began its trek through the San Gabriel Valley, taking both Stores Number 1 and Number 4 with it. The government bought the land and demolished the buildings. Harry took the money from the sale and purchased a large section of land near the site of the original Number 1 and immediately built a new store. He also bought a lot on Ramona Boulevard in West Covina, building a store there too. Remarkably, both Stores Number 1 and Number 4 were able to close one night and reopen the next day in their new locations—with no interruption in service.

That same year our iconic In-N-Out arrow made its first appearance on our signs, replacing the original "No Delay" design. Today we use two phrases referencing that motif: "We all work under the same arrow" and "The arrow points to pride."

In 1958, fountain service replaced bottles. Customers could choose Pepsi-Cola, Nesbitt's Orange, or Hires Root Beer. Each twelve-ounce cup (without a lid) cost ten cents.

Cool Cups

In 1958, Harry Snyder and a national cup company developed an agreement that In-N-Out Burger would use cups with red hearts and that the cup company wouldn't sell that version of the cup to other restaurants in our area.

A few years after Harry's death, the red-heart cups began to show up in nearby areas, so Rich Snyder called to remind the company of their arrangement. He was told that the previous agreement was with Harry, who was no longer at the helm. Rich decided a different cup vendor would get In-N-Out's business. In Harry's honor, Rich created the ubiquitous palm-tree cup design we still use today.

A store associate stands before an In-N-Out location
in Pomona, California, in the early 1960s.

In 1959, we opened a store at (notice the street name) 780 Arrow Highway, Covina, California. This store was dubbed Store Number 2 since it replaced the Number 2 that went to Charlie in the split. The new Store Number 2 was small—just one grill and two fryers. Chuck Papez, the youth who had bought his first car with Harry's help, was named manager.

At first, business was slow enough that Harry left Chuck to run Store Number 2 without oversight. Chuck was highly personable, and if a customer came in, he invited them to eat right there so he'd have someone to talk to. Word spread, and customers responded to Chuck's people skills as well as the signature quality of In-N-Out. The store soon became an In-N-Out Burger powerhouse. By 1974, Store Number 2, still under Chuck's management, set a new sales record, selling 56,808 burgers in one month.

Harry's wish to replace Store Number 3 was fulfilled in 1962 when

Esther Snyder with Bob Lang Sr. and Chuck Papez,
two of In-N-Out Burger's original associates who made
lasting leadership influences on the company.

In-N-Out Burger opened a store at 2450 Towne Avenue in Pomona.§
Business at this store also started out slowly. Sometimes business was so
slow that no sales were made from 9:00 p.m. to closing. But Harry stuck to
his established principles, and business at the store eventually grew.

While the day-to-day business of running the restaurant was Harry's
job, Esther became In-N-Out's heart. By all accounts she was gracious and
welcoming to customers, helpers, and vendors. She was a person of strong
faith, and while Harry didn't share her beliefs about God at the start, Esther
consistently practiced what she believed.

She developed a reputation for paying every bill upon receipt and mailing it out that night, believing that paying promptly showed respect to the vendors. If a vendor showed up at the door with an invoice, Esther wrote a check on the spot. Even when market conditions fluctuated, creating dips or rises in pricing, my grandparents stayed faithful to their vendors. Those suppliers, in turn, took care of In-N-Out.

To this day we take our vendor relationships very seriously. To even get in the running as a vendor for In-N-Out, a company must satisfy every one of In-N-Out's strict requirements, which can take more than a year. In-N-Out considers only the top companies of their fields as potential suppliers, and once a company becomes qualified and certified, In-N-Out becomes one of their best customers.

Esther promptly paid In-N-Out's helpers, too, and they loved her for it. Bob Lang Sr. was one of those young men. "Esther was a sweetheart," he recalled fondly. "She was like a mom. We were her 'boys.' It wasn't only that we were paid on time; we felt valued and respected."

Birth of Icons

Expansion meant that Harry needed to hire and train store managers. He saw this as a good step for business. He knew that to develop loyal helpers he needed to provide them with promotions, more responsibility, and more pay. He wanted his young hires to not only be able to afford cars but also be able to buy houses, get married, and start families.

In the beginning, when he sensed that someone was ready for a manager position, he'd invite them across the street to his house. There he gave them a small leather notebook with tabs for use as a manual. The notebook was blank inside, but Harry would instruct the new manager to copy a series of detailed instructions into the notebook. He believed that hearing a message, then writing it down, would give every manager an extra advantage.

Instructions were about how to serve customers great burgers, fries, and drinks. Details included how to correctly toast buns, how to clean the store, how to train helpers to be friendly to customers, how to create a daily report, and more. This was Harry's way of passing along In-N-Out's foundational principles.

Managers referred to the notebook system as "Harry's bible." These days, original copies are rare since the practice ended when Harry died, although most of the basics that he taught his managers are followed to this day.

Strangely, coffee preparation required more instructions than any other subject. The Dutch love their coffee. Providing customers with the perfect cup of coffee was extremely important to Harry. And he enjoyed it personally. Harry was almost always busy, but if ever a rare break in customer traffic occurred, he'd pour himself a cup, take it out to the picnic table at Store Number 1, and sip it for a few moments before heading back to work. He enjoyed sharing the coffee experience too. He invited police officers to stop by anytime for complimentary coffee. He believed frequent visits from law enforcement were good for business.

It's not that In-N-Out customers needed policing. But right from the beginning, In-N-Out Burger became the cool place to be, and all types of people were welcomed at our stores. Late at night young people often hung out in our parking lots for hours after going through the drive-thru. In the 1950s hot rods, Elvis, and greasers were a big part of popular culture, as were the beatniks, a bohemian counterculture movement that saw a lot of traction in Los Angeles's Venice West neighborhood. In the 1960s, hippies frequented our stores. The hot rod traffic never slowed. Surfer culture, with the Beach Boys and Jan and Dean, has always been a big part of Southern California ambiance, and many customers would grab a burger en route to or returning from the beach.

According to our historian, guys and their dates often hung out on the lots late at night. Many times they were friends of the young men who worked inside, but the guys outside would honk their horns while orders were taken, just to mess with their buddies. Or they'd leave trash on the lots and play their music extra loud. Occasionally they would get into fights. Good-naturedly, the helpers inside referred to them as "animals."

When business finished for the night, helpers were sometimes known to use In-N-Out ingredients to make customized burgers for themselves. One night in 1961, one of the animals from the lot asked Theo Roberts, then a third manager at Store Number 1, what kind of burger he was making for himself.

"It's mustard fried," Theo said. "I add pickles, grilled onions, and extra spread."

"Sounds amazing," the guy said. "Can you make me one too?"

Theo did, and the guy wolfed it down. The next night, the guy came back. "Wow, that was the best burger I've ever had," he said. "How do you order it?"

Theo shrugged. It wasn't on the menu. But he made him the same styled burger anyway. The guy came back night after night. After several nights of him asking how to order it, Theo looked at him and said, "Just call it Animal Style."

That's how Animal Style burgers got their name, and the request is the first known instance of a secret In-N-Out menu item. Today cheeseburgers, hamburgers, Double-Doubles, and fries can all be ordered Animal Style. We mustard-fry a beef patty, then add hand-leafed lettuce and tomato, pickle, extra spread, and grilled onions. Even though our menu has stayed the same for decades, secret menu items are often requested. It's amazing how many variations people come up with. As far as we know, Animal Style fries were first requested at Store Number 4 in West Covina in 2002. (Animal Style fries have melted cheese, grilled onion, and spread, but not all the burger ingredients.)

The iconic In-N-Out lap mats that customers know today were handed out to customers almost from the beginning, in 1948 or 1949, although the early mats looked different. Freshly baked buns came to the store wrapped in brown wax paper. Harry cut the paper into chunks and handed out a mat with each order so customers wouldn't drop food on their clothes as they ate in their cars. In 1961, Harry made the lap mats official, switching to pink butcher paper. He believed the pink paper made dining even more appealing on the bench seats common to cars of the era.

In 1966, Harry asked Bob Lang Sr. to create an official employee handbook (managers still used the "Harry's bible" method). Bob wrote one up, Harry okayed it, then Bob took it to the printer to have multiple copies made. The printer was a regular vendor who frequented In-N-Out himself.

"Just curious," the printer said. "Why do you hand out blank paper with each meal? You have high-quality products. You could tell your customers all about it on each mat."

Bob took the idea back to Harry, who loved it. A new tradition was born. The earliest printed lap mats featured maps noting the eight In-N-Out locations in existence at the time, plus the managers' names. Customers often tucked the "maps" into their glove boxes to help navigate their way around town—and to the next In-N-Out location. Since then, lap mats have been used to educate customers about various aspects of our fresh, high-quality food. We've also had a chance to let customers know about our charities, what they do, and why they do it.

For a few years customers had been ordering burgers with more than one patty, although they weren't on the menu. Some customers liked their burgers with both double meat and double cheese. Sometime in the early years, these began to be called Double-Doubles. An announcement for the

The Double-Double burger bag from 1990.

Double-Double debuted on a banner at Store Number 3 when it was located in Pomona. The Double-Double first appeared on the menu during the opening of Store Number 6 on August 1, 1966.

Highs and Lows

A strong sense of teamwork existed among the In-N-Out associates from the start, and the atmosphere in all the stores was always friendly. Behind the scenes there was never a question of who was in charge. Harry didn't suffer any foolishness. According to early associate Joe Gee, "You always knew where you stood with Harry. If you messed up, he'd yell. But ten minutes later everything would be fine."[6]

The teamwork forged in the tiny, early In-N-Out kitchens continues as a part of that legacy found in any In-N-Out kitchen today. The leadership style has changed, but that bond of working with teammates in a fun, fast-paced environment is a formative piece of our company culture.

Those who knew my grandfather best appreciated his accomplishments. He cared about people deeply, and he wanted to serve customers only the best. He excelled as a mentor, and he helped many people establish successful careers at In-N-Out. Still, those closest to him agreed that he had two faults. First, he'd developed a habit of smoking when he was a teen, a habit he never shook. He'd started in the era before the health risks of smoking were widely known, and he smoked a lot. Early In-N-Out stores even had cigarette machines. Second, every once in a while Harry's yelling became too much. Sometimes it was almost as if Harry reached back to his military days and ran things like a boot camp. Working for him meant you did what you were told and tried your best to stay out of trouble. He expected you to work the way he did: never miss a day of work, never make a mistake, and work as hard as possible.

At his best Harry ensured every customer's meal was prepared and served precisely to his high standards. There's no doubt in my mind that my grandfather was a perfectionist and a workaholic. He wanted to manage every aspect of the store experience to ensure happy customers. After In-N-Out had grown into several stores, he routinely popped into a kitchen unannounced to ask, "Is everything under control?" This was shorthand for, "Is everyone here in a position to serve the next customer the very highest quality meal to the very best of our ability?"

Cooks began to anticipate his question—almost as if Harry was on their shoulder ready to ask it at any time. It became his catchphrase. The question must've passed Harry's lips a million times, and at its best, it's a great question to ask.

The problem was that both of Harry's faults would eventually catch up with him.

Chapter Four

REDEMPTION

God so loved the world that He gave His one
and only Son, that whoever believes in Him
should not perish but have everlasting life.

JOHN 3:16

FOR A WHILE, AT LEAST ON THE SURFACE, EVERYTHING APPEARED TO be going smoothly. Certainly, the family business was doing well, with its loyal and growing customer base, and the Snyder family grew along with it. My father, Harry Guy Snyder, was born in 1951, followed quickly by my uncle Richard in 1952. Harry maintained his focus on running the company. My grandmother stepped out of day-to-day store business to raise their two sons, although she kept doing the books. She would return to full-time work at In-N-Out when they were teens.

Family home-video footage taken in the 1960s shows Harry and Esther smiling with their two children. A favorite photograph shows my dad and my uncle when they were little kids. They're sitting in a boat, both wearing captain hats. My dad sits behind the wheel, smiling, pretending to drive. Rich is sitting next to him, looking steadily at the camera with a smile. My grandparents are standing next to the boat, both smiling.

When I was a child, I spent a lot of time with my grandmother, who I soon learned embodied the description in Proverbs 31: a godly woman

In-N-Out's Founder, Harry Snyder with wife, Esther, and son, Rich Snyder.

with a noble character, respected, hardworking, and loved by all who knew her. While Harry could be rough, Esther was truly a sweetheart. Those who knew Harry best noted that he struggled with the responsibilities of fatherhood, particularly behind closed doors. To understand him, we need to look at the reasons. Harry's father had abused him when he was a child, to the point where young Harry had been locked in a closet and not fed. He'd never been shown how to become an exemplary father, and his own childhood abuse had never been dealt with. He was not given the love a child should have from his father, and the lack of acceptance and never feeling good enough was a pain he carried until the day he died.

My father, who went by his middle name, Guy, was an independent thinker from the start. He was headstrong and capable, a challenger, and he didn't respond well to illogical authority. He stood up to his father whenever they disagreed. Many say Guy had a bit of a rebellious streak.

Rich, the younger brother, saw the punishment Guy received by exerting independence and was eager to avoid trouble. He became the peacekeeper—went with the flow and tried to get along. If both boys got into trouble, Guy became protective of his little brother. Much of the time he took the blame to keep Rich from getting punished.

For years that's how things went in the Snyder household. Harry and Esther were successful businesspeople. But life at home was sometimes rocky.

When People Share

Meanwhile, with multiple locations steadily selling burgers, there was such a demand for patties that my grandparents opened a new patty-making facility in 1963. This allowed In-N-Out to provide an ever-increasing number of guests with traditional In-N-Out quality using the freshest ingredients available.

Though Store Number 4 had moved from El Monte to Ramona Boulevard in West Covina in 1954, it had one more move to make. In 1964, the local newspaper, the *San Gabriel Valley Tribune*, wanted to expand its facility and offered a direct exchange of their larger and more desirable piece of land for Store Number 4's property. That's why Store Number 4 moved about a half mile down the road to what is now the present location—a significantly busier one.*

The friendly atmosphere that Harry and Esther worked to cultivate at In-N-Out permeated the company. In 1967, Chuck Papez hired a seventeen-year-old high school student named Ed Pendleton. He spent his entire career

---

* Johnny Cassianni and Esley Fields comanaged that location in the early days.

at the company until his retirement. To this day, he loves and respects the company and Harry and Esther's legacy.

"You had to know somebody to get a job at In-N-Out back when I started," Ed recalled.

> These days, there might be a hundred people working at each store, but at that time each In-N-Out was a smaller box store with maybe fifteen or sixteen people working in each location. In-N-Out Burger was a small group of people then. Everybody worked together and knew each other.
>
> The Snyders were good about listening to their associates too. You have to understand what it takes to run a very successful business, where employees love working for you and want to be around you. We can all think of things we could do a little differently, but I can't say anything negative about the family. The Snyders shared everything they had. When people share like that, you're going to want to do everything you can to ensure they succeed.[1]

In 1968, Harry opened Store Number 7 in La Puente on Amar Road. As the new decade began in 1970, the small company was growing fast. In the next five years In-N-Out would more than double in size. In addition to the teams in each store, several people started working from the Snyder home office. Esther went back to work full time doing accounting and payroll.[†]

Soon Harry opened Store Number 9 in North Hollywood and Store Number 10 in Panorama City, both in the San Fernando Valley. Harry wanted his son Rich, who was about twenty by then, to learn how the stores should be operated, so Rich went to work with general manager Bob Williams at Number 9 and Number 10. Rich took naturally to learning

---

† In 1970, Ralph Harpster served as general manager. Pete Cogliaro made the spread and was in charge of landscaping, among other things. Delbert Morgan oversaw maintenance and new construction. For many years Delbert was our builder of stores and maintenance supervisor.

The 25th Anniversary Burger bag from 1973.

how to run the business. Harry sensed that one day his younger son would run the company.

Harry Delegates

One of my grandfather's favorite movies was the classic 1963 comedy *It's a Mad, Mad, Mad, Mad World* starring a string of that era's biggest stars: Spencer Tracy, Milton Berle, Ethel Merman, Mickey Rooney, Sid Caesar, Buddy Hackett, and Jonathan Winters. In the movie, contestants race to find treasure that's buried under four palm trees planted to resemble the letter *W*. Harry loved the movie so much that in 1972, as an homage, we started a tradition of planting two crossed palm trees in front of most In-N-Out locations. As in the movie, when you see the crossed palms, you've spotted the treasure.

More About Our Iconic Crossed Palm Trees

Why palm trees? Harry Snyder had a friend who owned several Sizzler Restaurants and who said to him, "You're starting to get popular and you need some sort of symbol that people can identify your restaurants with." At that time we had thirteen stores and Harry began to think about coming up with a symbol. He brainstormed ideas with Esther and the boys before coming up with the iconic palm trees we have today.

What type of palm trees do we plant? Bob Williams, who later became vice president of operations, revealed that the first palms Harry planted (at Store Number 2 in Covina, California) were the large, round ones that do not grow much. Harry then went with the *Washingtonia robusta*, also known by other names such as the Mexican fan palm, Mexican Washingtonia, or Skyduster. This species of palm tree is native to Baja California, Mexico.

We continue to use palm trees as our symbol to this day. But we faced challenges in the past when trying to achieve the desired crossed appearance. Initially we planted the palms at an angle and hoped they would naturally cross as they grew larger, but this strategy was unsuccessful. Next we attempted to grow them and then cross them when they got bigger, but this approach also failed. Currently we purchase two twenty-foot Mexican Fan palm trees and manually cross them at a height of ten feet. They look great! Most of our stores have crossed palm trees, and fifteen stores even have two sets. Keep your eyes out for them next time you visit an In-N-Out Burger!

With the number of stores and managers increasing, Harry finally felt he could relax a bit. He knew the continued success of In-N-Out depended on sticking with the quality that had become its hallmark. His personal presence in the stores to offer feedback to cooks and teams had provided that constancy for years. But he couldn't do that forever. With a strong general manager in place, Bob Williams, Harry felt he could take a step back.

As he grew older, Harry wanted to be comfortable enough with the business to be able to play golf every day. In Southern California that's actually an option. Slowly, Harry began to delegate more. Chuck Papez was the first to run a store by himself. He managed Store Number 2 in Covina on Arrow Highway. In 1974, Harry tasked Chuck with traveling from store to store to ensure consistency of In-N-Out products, quality, service, and cleanliness. That position evolved into what's now the divisional manager role.

Harry needed this extra help, too, because it was only a matter of time before he would be unable to do it himself. As he entered his sixties, Harry spent more time playing golf, and eventually he achieved his personal dream of playing a round each day. But it wasn't all the sunny semiretirement he'd dreamed of. Sometimes he was short of breath. He wheezed and was constantly tired. He developed a cough that didn't go away. Harry and Esther grew concerned and started searching for answers.

Birth of Traditions

Meanwhile, the business kept moving forward. The first official In-N-Out cookout was held in Covina for Badillo Elementary School on December 7, 1974.

My uncle Rich, twenty-two by then, had received a letter from an elementary school teacher in Chino who'd assigned her class to write about what kind of inanimate object they'd most like to be and why. One student wanted to be a Double-Double. When Rich read the letter, he arranged to bring lunch to the class as a treat. But he didn't want the burgers cold by the time he arrived, so with the help of two associates, Chuck Papez and Ralph

Mark Taylor (left) working a Cookout event.

Harpster, he drove out in a pickup truck with a portable grill and a wooden salad table. From the tailgate, they cooked and prepared the burgers. The students were delighted.

The onetime event worked so well that it grew into a full program. As much as we love inviting customers into our stores, we also love bringing the In-N-Out experience to school events, churches, charities, weddings, birthday parties, and concerts. We're often at Oscar parties, on movie sets—you name it. Today we have twenty fully self-supported Cookout Trucks and 125 mobile team members, all poised and ready to serve. The "trucks" are

fun FACT

If you'd like to schedule a cookout truck, see our Insider Info. You plan the event. We'll cook the burgers.[2]

actually more like big rigs—the tractors that pull the trailers are converted from semis. The trailers are custom-built rolling kitchens.

We currently service all of Los Angeles and Orange County as well as limited parts of Ventura, San Bernardino, and Riverside Counties. We also service limited parts of the Dallas–Fort Worth Metroplex, Denver, Colorado Springs, and Las Vegas.

I've been to many cookouts, and it's such fun to see people's faces light up when they see the In-N-Out Cookout Truck arrive. Our mobile team has helped us grow in our ability to serve when nobody else can or will, even when natural disasters hit our communities. We've engaged the cookout trucks to show appreciation for firefighters and first responders, whom we enjoy giving back to whenever possible.

The Rose Parade is an annual tradition broadcast on national television for as long as I can remember. In 1974, we fired up those portable

The holiday burger bag from 1974.

grills for the first time at the Tournament of Roses Parade in Pasadena. We've been serving thousands of people at the Rose Bowl Parade ever since.

Today In-N-Out feeds all the Rose Bowl Tournament bands at Band Fest prior to the parade (December 29 and 30) and at the end of the Rose Parade on New Year's Day—plus both football teams in the Rose Bowl at the Team Feed. In 2022 we served about fifteen thousand burgers there.

On May 5, 1974, our signature red aprons were introduced in all our stores, replacing the white aprons we'd had since opening in 1948. Harry always liked a white uniform with black shoes and belt because it showed cleanliness. But the red aprons gave each In-N-Out associate a pop of color that had long been associated with the In-N-Out brand. Harry acquiesced. From the company's start we had called our entire uniforms "whites," a tradition that continues. A manager might call up an associate during a particularly busy rush and say, "I need you right away. Get in your whites." It just seems respectful of the tradition.

History of the Apron Pin

When Harry founded In-N-Out, he chose a classic white waist apron to complement the white shirts and pants of the dress uniform. Unlike those in most establishments, however, his aprons were secured with apron pins instead of drawstrings.

For many years In-N-Out helpers used diaper pins to secure their aprons. The pins were cheap and plentiful, as cloth diapers were a household norm throughout the 1950s and 1960s. Pins came in many colors, but our stores usually kept supplies of white-capped pins on hand in the desk drawer in the back room.

In the early 1960s, Harry began using linen services to wash the white uniforms. The linen company used large brass safety pins stamped with route numbers to secure the bags of linen. Later they used plain pins and would attach a metal circle with the store number. These pins became highly prized by helpers, as they looked more professional and were sturdier than diaper pins.

In 1973, with the opening of the new Baldwin Park warehouse, the larger pin—now brass with a silver coating—was issued to all new associates. Stores continued to have diaper pins in stock into the early 1980s—just in case a pin was lost or borrowed by another associate.

By 1975, just past the quarter-century mark of the company's existence, In-N-Out had grown to eighteen stores. All were in Los Angeles County except for Number 17 in Santa Ana, which is in Orange County. All our restaurants were two-lane by then (double-lane drive-thru stores). No dining-room stores had been built yet, although a few had small tables outside for guests.

Harry kept working. And he kept golfing. And he kept coughing.

fun FACT

Associates once used the pins as key chains, a tradition started by Harry. It was common to see keys on the apron pins until the early 1980s. Rich decided on a more consistent look, so he made it policy that the pin be unadorned.

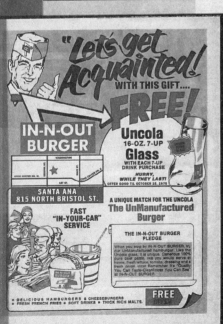

WHAT IS AN IN-N-OUT FRENCH FRY?

First, it is a Grade 1 fresh potato — peeled and sliced at each location. Potatoes are peeled a few hours before cooking. The oil is a pure vegetable oil used for cooking our fries to order.

Towels are used for drying off the oil. Be member when using a fresh potato, it may not look quite as consistent as a frozen fry—but the flavor you taste is the fresh potato, not nothing oil.

With portion controls of frozen foods being sold to restaurants today, we are one of the few still selling a fresh potato.

STORE #17
Store Location: Santa Ana, CA
Opening Date: September 28, 1975
Opening Mgr. *Steve Denny*

...e second-to-last *In-N-Out Burger* opened by our founder, ... 1975, it was the first *In-N-Out* in Orange County. Like all ... as a single-grill, two-lane restaurant. It was Harry's vision ... ld serve the freshest, highest quality hamburgers, with ... an stores.

...ery few *In-N-Out Burger* locations built with a basement. ... ode prevented the hand-leafed lettuce and freshly sliced ... oss the drive lane into the kitchen (or "stand") from the ... downstairs and carried upstairs many times each day. ... the backroom, so buckets of freshly-peeled potatoes ... as they were needed for dicing.

...d on Sunday, July 12, 2020, Store #17 was closed for a ...ened in early 2021, the "new" Store #17 is located just ...

...one, more available parking and a larger patio area, and ...low more customers to pull in off of Bristol Avenue. The ...prepared in the same building as the "stand," but there is ...toes are still stored and peeled in the backroom and ...'re needed.

...nal Store #17 served fresh, high quality hamburgers and ...lmost 45 years. With that kind of wonderful support, our ...for generations to come.

Store #17
Sunday, September 28, 1975

Our first store located in Orange County!
This brick was saved from the original building.

A display case at Store Number 17 in Santa Ana showcases items from when the location first opened in 1975.

The Curious Case of Store Number 17

At the time of Harry Snyder's passing in 1976, all eighteen of his In-N-Out Burger stores were double-drive or two-lane stores. In Orange County a zoning ordinance caused Harry to depart from the traditional design pioneered at Store Number 5 (the oldest remaining store in its original location). The ordinance said that ready-to-eat product could not be transported across an open space. This meant items such as pans of hand-leafed lettuce and inserts of sliced tomatoes and onions could not be prepared in a separate back room, then brought across the back lane into the kitchen, as happened at every other store.

Harry's solution was to construct the store in Santa Ana (opened on September 27, 1975) with a basement, the first store to have this feature. This allowed associates to prepare lettuce, tomatoes, and onions indoors, then carry them up the staircase into the stand. Though the original staircase was located right behind the fry station, the open stairwell was later moved for safety reasons. Otherwise the basic layout of this store was like other stores.

The basement was built directly under the kitchen, which was elongated to provide room for the staircase. The walk-up window, traditionally placed at the center of the back wall, had to be moved closer to the front lane and was enclosed for safety reasons. There wasn't room for dining tables, but there was some indoor space for customers—a first in company history.

Store Number 17 has since been remodeled. It features a second grill and a huge drive lane, which will allow it to continue to serve Orange County customers at a high level for many years to come.

Four Fun Facts About Store Number 17

1. The beautiful, remodeled Store Number 17 opened in April 2021.
2. It features a second grill and unique display case with items from when the first store opened in 1975.
3. The remodeled kitchen area is big enough to handle food prep, so the basement is no longer needed.
4. An extra lot was purchased so the drive lanes could be lengthened; the extended lanes now fit thirty-five cars.

Constant Cars and Burgers

To work at In-N-Out in the 1940s through 1970s, you needed to know your cars because orders were still called out verbally since modern point-of-sale systems hadn't been invented yet. Associates called out each customer's order by noting the make, model, color, or year of their car. Day and night, shouts rang across the kitchen: "Double-Double, fries, and a Coke for the red Mustang. Two strawberry shakes and a cheeseburger no onions for the green Dodge Dart!"

Car watching was fun—and working in a drive-thru gave helpers a chance to experience and admire lots of different makes and models. I grew up appreciating a well-made machine, so I understand this 100 percent.

Back in 1965, when my dad was fourteen, my grandfather had invested in the Irwindale Raceway, formalizing an existing connection between In-N-Out and classic cars. At the racetrack, hungry racers and fans could buy

PLAY THE GAME
CRUISE IN-N-WIN!
© 1997 In-N-Out Burgers, a California Corporation.

The "Cruise In-N-Win" was a promotional In-N-Out giveaway that offered customers chances to win prizes worth up to a new car.

In-N-Out burgers from the concession stands staffed mostly by off-duty In-N-Out workers. The unbranded burgers were served with no tomatoes for reasons lost to history. Harry paid In-N-Out workers a premium to work the snack bars at Irwindale because he knew they could deliver the kind of food he wanted to serve. Though the burgers sold at Irwindale weren't branded as In-N-Out, he used the same ingredients and the same methods that created such a devoted following at In-N-Out stores. The delicious burgers became part of the racetrack experience.

Classic cars, muscle cars, drag racing—they're an indelible part of In-N-Out's culture and history. From the earliest drive-thru-only stores where car enthusiasts showed off their cool cars, to our part ownership in and presence at Irwindale Raceway, to several family members drag racing, to our partnership with In-N-Out Burger Pomona Dragstrip, to the final national event of the year on the National Hot Rod Association circuit—the In-N-Out Burger NHRA Finals held at Pomona—yes, all this makes it clear that In-N-Out people are car people.

Harry Goes Home

In-N-Out's cofounder, the driving force behind the company, had entered his last season of life. Harry's thirty years of smoking had done its damage. Near the beginning of 1975, the coughing and shortness of breath he was experiencing was formally diagnosed as lung cancer. And it was bad. Doctors could not give him an optimistic prognosis.

Harry fought cancer with everything he had. He endured chemotherapy. His hair fell out. He underwent multiple medical treatments stateside and even went to Mexico for experimental treatment. For a short while it looked like the cancer was going into remission. Then it returned. Soon Harry coughed all the time. Sometimes he coughed up blood. His voice turned permanently hoarse, then dimmed to a whisper. Finally he understood that he wasn't going to beat this.

Esther had prayed for him for years, but Harry had never turned to God in any meaningful way. She talked to her husband seriously—and urgently. He had created the In-N-Out concept and menu, built and managed eighteen thriving locations in Southern California, fostered a loyal customer base, and found like-minded, friendly apprentices to work alongside him, people whom he had mentored well. He worked hard, saved money, bought the right properties, and, together with my grandmother, built a trusted, thriving family business. But she knew that he still needed to make sure things were right between him and his Maker. Harry needed to be ready to meet God.

As the end neared, Harry made sure his business in this world was in order. He named my uncle, Rich, as president and my dad as vice president. Though the brothers were young—just twenty-four and twenty-five—they knew the business well, having grown up immersed in the company. They'd seen firsthand the hard work and faithful dedication it took to make In-N-Out successful.

At the eleventh hour, Esther's prayers were answered. As Harry lay propped in a semisitting position in bed, his breathing labored, his body exhausted, he bowed his head and trusted the promise of John 3:16, that

God loved him in spite of his faults. God loved him so much, in fact, that he'd sent Jesus to die on a cross—for Harry's sins as well as all mankind's. The promise offers that if anyone believes in this work of Jesus, he will have eternal life. Harry said yes.

Without a doubt, I know my grandfather is in heaven today. He accepted his Lord and Savior on his deathbed. Harry's life on earth ended on December 14, 1976. He was sixty-three years old. His funeral was held three days after his passing at the Forest Lawn Memorial Park and Mortuary in Covina Hills. Hundreds of people attended.

Had he lived perfectly? No. But he achieved much more in his lifetime than his own parents had ever dreamed. The integrity of Harry's vision never wavered. Under his care, In-N-Out had become a staple of Southern California life. Those who worked alongside Harry were his biggest fans.

Complications

Harry's story was not concluded with his death. Nearly eight years passed. Late one night in 1984, my uncle showed up unexpectedly at my father's place and asked to talk. It was long after the funeral. Long after all the goodbyes were said. Long after the man who'd given the world so much through his simple hamburger stand had been honored for the good he'd done in his life.

My uncle and my father sat, and Rich immediately teared up. "Guy," he said. "When we were kids, we were abused."

My father nodded. It was not news to him.

They knew that "abuse" is a strong word. Child abuse happens whenever a parent or caregiver, whether through action or failure to act, causes injury, death, emotional pain, or risk of serious harm to a child. Many forms of child abuse exist, including neglect, abandonment, physical abuse, sexual abuse, exploitation, and emotional abuse. The brothers started discussing their childhood pain.

The abuse that Rich and Guy experienced had been physical, mental, and emotional. Harry had been too tough on the kids, especially on Guy. Harry had such high expectations of himself and his stores, and his high expectations extended to his sons. But while Harry could articulate exactly what kind of results he expected in his stores, he had great difficulty in articulating what he hoped for his family.

His sons always had trouble knowing what might upset their father, always guessing, which made for a tumultuous relationship. Harry wasn't shy about yelling at them, and the boys were often afraid. One time when they were very young, Harry bought them toys then threatened to give away those toys if they were "bad." The boys did something that Harry didn't like. The particulars are lost, but what they'd done was probably not much different than things most kids do. There was the usual sibling rivalry, bickering, and fighting between the brothers. Harry followed through on his threat and gave away their new toys. The reasons were never made clear to Rich and Guy.

Harry had strict rules about food and didn't allow the boys to eat candy at home. He allowed sweets if the boys' aunt offered them some during a visit, but otherwise sweets were strictly forbidden. Once, my dad climbed a fence and shimmied through a window into a neighbor's house. He was just a little kid, and all he wanted was a cookie. A container of salt fell from a cabinet. Salt flew into the boy's eyes, causing them to sting intensely. Harry discovered the transgression and inflicted more pain on his son at home.

Punishment, for Guy and Rich, usually meant being hit with a ruler or sometimes a yardstick. These weren't swats or even spankings, like many children received who grew up in that era. These were beatings. When it came to using the ruler, Harry always offered a choice: wood or metal? If Guy was by himself, he chose wood, although the strokes would hurt just as much as metal. Harry would beat the boys until a wooden ruler broke. If Guy and Rich were being punished at the same time, Guy chose metal. That way the older brother left the younger brother the wooden ruler. Guy hated for Rich to get hurt. Once the wooden ruler broke, the beating was over.

Of the two brothers, Guy repeatedly experienced the worst abuse. He often maneuvered the situation so he could take on Rich's punishment. Over time Guy became the family scapegoat, so much that when he was twelve, Harry sent him to Brown's Military Academy, a strict military boarding school.

My father lived away from home for all of middle school. The institution was only a few miles away from the Snyder house, but Harry made his son board on campus. My father told me once that his years at boarding school were some of the most painful times of his life. He felt neglected and abandoned. It wasn't merely that the school was strict or that he was away from home. Harry wanted him isolated to teach him a lesson. When other kids' parents came to visit on the weekends, young Guy waited, hoping his family would come. Many times he cried when they didn't come.

Harry was not known to be a cruel person outside of his home. It's difficult to say exactly why he did what he did. Given his own abusive upbringing, I think my grandfather had never known anything different. It wasn't that he did everything wrong as a parent. Dad and Uncle Rich enjoyed a lot of time during their formative years at the Irwindale Raceway. Harry often took them there, and in a way, that's where my dad's lifelong passion for cars and racing took hold.

My father returned home after boarding school and went to a regular high school, although he continued in his rebellious ways. In auto shop class, Guy was assigned an engine rebuilding project with a buddy named Jeff Helmrich, who'd grown up in a boys' home. Guy and Jeff found a junked engine, rebuilt it, and got it to run. After graduating, Jeff went to work for In-N-Out. He tells of some of the boys' late-night activities.

> We could be a bit cantankerous back in high school. We would work on our cars all day. Sometimes we got them to where they would run pretty good. Around midnight we'd be ready to test out these cars on Cypress Avenue. We would discreetly drive away, really quietly, and do our "testing" down the street. Really, it was illegal street racing. When we came back hours later, we'd put the car in neutral, shut off the engine and headlights, and coast in.

Mrs. Snyder would be standing at the door of the garage asking us, "Are you boys alright?"

I was thinking, *How did you know we took off?* Years later I asked Mrs. Snyder how she always knew we were out racing. Turns out she had a friend on Cypress who'd call her up and say, "The boys are racing again."[3]

Redemption

Rich and Guy had a complicated upbringing. As they talked that night in 1984, they confessed some of their own feelings of hurt they held toward each other. While my father loved his brother, he held some resentment and jealousy. He envied his younger brother because he thought Rich got babied. Rich had never been abandoned or neglected like my dad. Likewise, my uncle felt hurt by my dad. He was jealous of his popularity in school, his carefree attitude, his ability to work on cars. I remember my uncle saying he loved how my dad was more of a free spirit. Dad never cared much what people thought about him. Rich was always more concerned about his reputation. They both had reasons to envy each other.

To the best of our family's knowledge, Harry had never been confronted about his abuse. He never offered any apologies. I don't know exactly what my grandmother thought about the events at home, or if she even knew. Harry had asked God to forgive him on his deathbed, and maybe he would have done more toward reconciliation if he hadn't passed so soon after he turned his life over to Christ.

People sometimes wonder why God allows painful situations to happen, including child abuse. The answer is that God has given people free will, and sometimes, tragically, people exercise their free will in horrible ways. Particularly when they have been wounded, they can act out of their pain and hurt others in return.

The ultimate answer to our pain and suffering is that God heals us and makes us new. God sent his only Son, Jesus, to die on the cross as a sacrifice for the sins of the world. Because of Jesus' work on the cross, people are able to be truly healed and have a new life. Second Corinthians 5:17 says, "Therefore, if anyone is in Christ, he is a new creation; old things have passed away; behold, all things have become new." If we have been harmed by someone else, we don't have to act out of our pain and hurt others in return. Patterns of abuse certainly do not need to be repeated.

In fact, if something bad has happened to us, God can turn that around and use it for good, so we can help others. In 2 Corinthians 1:4 the Bible says that God "comforts us in all our troubles, so that we can comfort those in any trouble with the comfort we ourselves receive from God" (NIV). If we've been hurt, our pain can be redeemed. Our hurts can be redeemed and used for good to help others.

That's exactly what my uncle and my father experienced that night in 1984, when everything was laid on the table. Something redemptive was born. Within days they started the Child Abuse Fund, today called the In-N-Out Burger Foundation.

More than seven hundred thousand documented cases of child abuse occur each year in America.[4] Yes, it's that widespread—and it's that tragic. Every ten seconds a child abuse report is placed. The In-N-Out Burger Foundation's purpose is to assist children who have been victims of child abuse and to prevent others from suffering the same way. Foundation funds provide emergency shelter, residential treatment, foster care, and early intervention for children in need.

Esther helped start the foundation, and my mother, Lynda Snyder, was very much involved in the early years. Her husband, my dad, had been abused, and it got her thinking of other kids and how she wanted to make a difference in their lives. My mom is organized, artistic, very giving, and eager to help.

Originally the funds came from annual can drives in stores. Customers would drop any amount of money into cans at the cash register of In-N-Out Burger stores. Today we still hold the can drives in January (National Human Trafficking Prevention Month), April (National Child Abuse Prevention Month), and October (National Substance Abuse Prevention Month). Online donations are also accepted. During each respective month, we match all donations three to one. In 1987, we held our first Children's Benefit Golf Tournament for vendors, associates, and supporters to raise funds for the In-N-Out Burger Foundation. It's now a much-anticipated annual event.

To this day In-N-Out pays 100 percent of the foundation's administrative costs so that every cent raised goes directly to centers providing help to abused children—resulting in millions of dollars of investment in children's lives.

Every person is precious and created in God's image. This work is so important to me. At In-N-Out, we firmly believe that with the help of our customers and others, we can create awareness and help prevent the unconscionable act of child abuse. We can change the startling facts that go with it. We can give a voice, and a hopeful chance, to abused children everywhere. Together, we can make a difference.

Chapter Five

THE ERA OF UNCLE RICH

"A new commandment I give to you, that
you love one another; as I have loved
you, that you also love one another."

John 13:34

AS I MENTIONED, MY UNCLE RICH WAS ONLY TWENTY-FOUR YEARS old in 1976 when he became the second official president of In-N-Out Burger. He was so capable that it looked like everything might go well, but in my experience life can throw curveballs.

Rich at the helm pleased both his mother and brother. Even though he was older, my dad didn't want the job, particularly at first. At the time of Harry's death, Esther was only fifty-six and a capable businesswoman, but she didn't want to assume the reins either. She and my grandfather had discussed succession before Harry had died. Esther worked closely with the vendors, valued those relationships, and wanted to keep on as she'd been doing.

Besides, having Rich run the company made sense. Although he hadn't attended college, he knew the business inside and out and had been mentored in management at In-N-Out for years. Harry had even involved Rich in intricate parts of the business, such as fighting trademark and copyright infringements. So Esther kept her title of secretary-treasurer as well as her controlling interest in the company. My dad, age twenty-five, found his

Esther Snyder with son Rich Snyder.

sweet spot as vice president. Rich was poised to lead the company into its next era. So far, so good.

Though Harry had positioned the transition to go well, his sons were impacted by his death in different ways. Rich wanted to succeed professionally in the business world and eagerly took the reins. Guy cared about the company and his family, but he preferred working on engines and racing cars.

Growing up, both boys had spent a lot of time at Irwindale Raceway. But Harry had ended the family's business interest in the raceway just before his death, with Rich's full support. This swung the focus back to food. But the move hurt my father. For him, racing was more than a business decision—it was his passion. He dreamed of creating a safe place for people to race, and he believed it helped get teens off the streets and channel their energy into something positive. On the heels of losing his father, for Guy the loss of the family's formal connection to the dragstrip must have felt like a punch to the gut. (For more on the historic relationship between In-N-Out and Irwindale, see "Insider Info #4: In-N-Out Burger and Irwindale Raceway.")

Guy and Rich agreed, however, on the main issues. They wanted to honor their mother and preserve In-N-Out Burger's legacy. They didn't want to sell the company or franchise the business. They were committed to excellence just as Harry had been. They believed in treating all associates well and paying them more than industry standards. They believed the customer always came first. Rich and Guy had learned the business by working and serving alongside their father. They'd seen Harry build and maintain eighteen stores. Now the reputation and future of all he'd built was in their hands.

In a video recording made in the 1980s, my grandmother said, "My two boys, Rich and Guy, they had to do what their father said, and sometimes they didn't care about that. But he instilled in them the right things to run In-N-Out. Those two boys really learned a lot from their dad. I look at them and see certain qualities each one had from their father. They're good workers and I'm real proud of Guy and Rich."[1]

Fire in the Sky

If Rich had any doubts about his ability to run the company at such a young age, he'd been assured of his father's belief in him. After Harry's funeral Rich stepped boldly into leadership, giving it 100 percent of his focus. He wanted to grow the company but do it strategically. My grandmother, especially, had his back. Rich and Esther were always close. Right from those early days of Rich's leadership, she threw her unwavering support his direction. Empowered by her support, Rich threw himself into the job at every level.

Early one morning, soon into Rich's tenure, a young associate named Ray Maldonado was working at Store Number 14 in Norwalk. When they received their daily delivery of produce, Ray noticed the tomatoes were underripe. He called the office and said, "We have a problem."

Forty-five minutes later, a Chevy El Camino pulled up. It was none other than In-N-Out's new president, my uncle Rich, delivering fresh produce himself.

"I knew we were in good hands that day," Ray said years later in an interview. "There was never a drop in the quality of product."[2]

Quality Spotlight: Bob Lang Jr.'s Recollection on the Importance of Pickles

The typical In-N-Out associate does not think about pickles much, if at all. Pickles are available on request, and Animal Style burgers include pickles. But because we do not have to prep pickles like we do our fresh produce items, we rarely think about them beyond resupplying them or placing them on the dressed bottom buns.

But Bob Lang Jr. learned they were never an afterthought. Bob tells the story of an event Rich hosted for second managers at the Baldwin Park warehouse in 1990 that changed his perspective.

I was with a group that was going to tour the warehouse. Rich was in the group. Rich was not the tour leader; it was somebody else with the warehouse, and they started leading the tour. But Rich could not contain himself.

We'd been on that tour for less than a minute when suddenly Rich took over as tour guide. "Now here are our tomatoes. These tomatoes, they are Aces, and they are the right size for our burger.

Service with a smile is a tradition at In-N-Out Burger.

They're the right taste and the best tomatoes you can buy." He talked about the buns. "They're made with a sponge dough and no preservatives and extra ingredients. We use malt and we use granulated sugar. These are the best buns you can buy."

He was taking us through all these items. Then he got to a pallet of pickles. To myself, I'm saying, *Okay, what's he going to say about pickles?* No sooner do I wonder that than Rich says, "These aren't just any pickles. We didn't just buy these off the shelf. We did a taste profile on these pickles. They have just the right crunchiness, the right flavor to go with our burger. These are a special In-N-Out pickle."

And I'm thinking, *Wow! Rich has thought of everything!* I was a divisional manager at the time. I remember being in awe of how he went around the warehouse that day. Rich had a passion for everything we do.

The moral of this story is simple: In-N-Out's passion for quality extends to every aspect of the customer experience. While we might not think much about pickles, rest assured the Snyder family has done the research into the very best choice. In fact, In-N-Out pickles are the best for our burgers!

Another longtime principle that Rich owned right from the start of his era was respect for every worker. Other restaurants might treat new employees as dispensable, but they were highly valued in Rich's eyes. Since the beginning, my grandfather had hired only the friendliest and most hardworking helpers. With training and mentoring, many stayed over the long haul. Those who had served customers faithfully for years became like family to the Snyders. It was a legacy Rich committed to continuing.

According to Mark Taylor, who worked for Rich near the start of his tenure, "Rich made us all feel so special and so proud to be a part of what we do. He was bigger than life, just a super guy."[3]

Bob Lang Jr., retired executive vice president of operations, agreed with that assessment. "Rich was always reminding us how important we were to him and to the success of In-N-Out," he said.[4]

Rich could be subtle about his methods for maintaining quality. He was known to quietly visit other restaurants to study how they did business. He saw firsthand that the freshest, highest quality foods matter, and that a good meal tastes even better when served by cheerful people. He observed that guests who are made to feel special enjoy their meal even more. He brought home the information to help reinforce our existing practices and sharpen In-N-Out even further. Friendly service and customer satisfaction had always been a priority for Harry. Rich inspired even greater levels of customer care.

One change that Rich soon made was to swap the official designation of In-N-Out employees from "helpers," as it had been under Harry, to "associates." He believed the new word sounded more professional. It communicated an increased sense of value and respect to employees. The new designation made sense now that the company was growing.

Rich had an eye on the future. He wanted In-N-Out to grow larger than Harry had ever dreamed. On June 25, 1978, only seven months after Harry's death, Rich opened Store Number 19 at 9032 Trask Avenue in Garden Grove.

A year after he began as president, Rich established the In-N-Out Training Department, appointing veteran In-N-Out manager Jack Ruley as training manager. Jack would be trusted to train others just as Harry had done for decades. Manager trainees were sent to Store Number 1 to learn from Jack. He'd have them open the store in the morning, run each shift, supervise cooking and cleanup, and complete each day's paperwork before closing for the night. Typically this took three days under Jack's watchful eye and close tutoring. Only when Jack was certain that a trainee was ready would that person be authorized to run an In-N-Out store.

Everything was running well. In-N-Out was a respected brand with a strong following of customers. Rich honored all the historic good in the company while stepping up to lead it to a new level.

But it couldn't all be smooth sailing.

On August 16, 1978, just eighteen months after Rich assumed leadership, an inspector from the US Department of Agriculture was scheduled to make his rounds at the In-N-Out headquarters at 13502 East Virginia Avenue in Baldwin Park, which was the company's hub of activity. Everything flowed through here. He would have inspected the warehouse and meat department and met with Rich in the on-site corporate office. He had his own inspection office, which was required at meat production facilities, and during his visit everything likely looked copacetic, as it always did. But sometime during that visit the inspector appears to have used the space heater in his provided office. Whether he simply flipped the heater on and off isn't known, but a heater definitely sat in that office.

Later that evening, after everybody had gone home, a spiral of smoke rose quietly from the In-N-Out headquarters. Those were the days before indoor sprinkler systems were mandated. Some unknown neighbor must have noticed the smoke and called the fire department. Sirens wailed. By the time firefighters arrived, an inferno raged. Fifty-five-gallon drums of cooking oil ignited and shot through the roof. Huge clouds of black smoke billowed into the sky.

The blaze ravaged the warehouse and corporate office space. The meat department, where meat was deboned, ground, and pattied for our burgers, was gutted. We made all our fresh patties here and shipped them to our other locations daily. We also lost the location where we made our spread, the area for cleaning uniforms, and the hub for product storage and shipment. Everything was destroyed, along with office documents, records, and precious family archives.

The wreckage smoldered a full week after the fire was extinguished. Fire inspectors traced the fire's origins to the space heater in the USDA inspector's on-site office.

It would take years to account for the losses, much less replace what was destroyed. The fire was a devastating blow because the building was very underinsured. How would my family and the In-N-Out associates keep it from being fatal?

Recovery and Growth

The fire could have shut us down for a long time. But Rich's unwavering leadership, plus decades of carefully cultivated relationships with vendors, plus managers and associates doubling down on hard work, saved the day. Rich vowed to keep every store open. He didn't want anybody to lose their job. He wanted to ensure that customers could still be served. If anyone doubted that Rich was up to the challenge, those doubts were put to rest when they saw him successfully lead through that crisis.

Vendors rallied to help our company. My grandparents had always been loyal to them, and now they returned that loyalty to In-N-Out. Supplies were delivered, and vendors went the extra mile to make sure our stores received exactly what they needed. A warehouse was immediately leased for interim use, and the small storage facility at Store Number 1 was enlisted. Esther lived in San Dimas then, and the day after the fire, she called the accounting associates into her home to work. Desks were set up in her living room. My dad set up his office in the guesthouse in her backyard. Somehow, despite the losses, the managers and associates at each In-N-Out store rose to the challenge and faithfully served top-quality burgers, fries, and drinks to customers as always. We didn't miss a beat.

Rich planned new headquarters in Baldwin Park, and even while rebuilding, he formulated dreams of expansion. On December 21, 1978, only four months after the fire, Rich opened Store Number 20 at 4242 North Rosemead Boulevard in Rosemead. In-N-Out was well on its way to recovery.

Less than a year later, on October 4, 1979, we opened Store Number 21 at 2235 Mountain Avenue in Ontario, California. This store's design departed from previous stores—and it would mark a new and exciting trend. For a long time, customers had given us feedback that they wanted to come inside In-N-Out and eat indoors. Number 21 was built with a dining room.

Store Number 21 became the first In-N-Out Burger to use a computerized point-of-sale register for customer transactions. Manager Keith Brazeau had previous experience with computers, and he implemented the system. In 1979, computers had been around for a while, but home computers were still a novelty. Most typing was still done on typewriters.

Using the register, associates entered each customer's order at the front counter or window. The info flowed to a printer in the kitchen where the associates prepared the order. In those early days, both the operating system and the database were loaded on tapes.* The operating system took ten minutes to load. Rich appreciated the new system and considered it an important step in modernizing our stores.

---

* In addition to Keith Brazeau's leadership, outstanding associates who started working for In-N-Out in the 1970s include Gary Murphy (1971–2021, divisional manager and QFC field evaluator), Phil West (1971–93, passed away as vice president of finance and administration), Wendell Ansnes (1971–2021, divisional manager, retired as QFC field evaluator), Greg Fairchild (1972–2019, retired as divisional manager), Keith Brazeau (1973–2018, retired as vice president of QFC), Rudy Mercado (1973–2020, retired as internal quality auditor), and Bob Lang Jr. (1973–2020, retired as executive vice president of operations). Dan Gimlett developed all the checklists and tests and color-coded the order-taking menu for our first point-of-sale computers.

The Story of the Flying Dutchman

At In-N-Out, the Flying Dutchman is a burger found on our not-so-secret menu: two meat patties, each with a slice of melted cheese, stacked on top of each other. Sometimes people hear the term and think about the ghost ships in the *Pirates of the Caribbean* movies or the cartoon character in SpongeBob SquarePants. But at In-N-Out, the association is about family and tradition.

By the time Guy Snyder was in high school (1965–69), Harry already had part ownership of the Irwindale Raceway. Having grown up in a car culture and spending time at the raceway, Guy loved working on and driving cars. With his love of racing and the race car circuit, and because Guy was proud of his Dutch heritage (one of his nicknames was Dutch), his natural racing nickname became the Flying Dutchman.

In the 1950–70s, cooks took orders verbally and memorized them. In those days all the cooks were managers, and the company was small enough that all the managers knew Guy and his racing nickname. Guy's signature burger order, two cooked cheese patties, became known as a Flying Dutchman because the associates had learned his order and it was easier for the cooks to remember.

In-N-Out grew much larger in the 1980s and early 1990s, and the use of a point-of-sale system changed how we operated. The phrase "Flying Dutchman" gradually faded from use in the In-N-Out vocabulary, to the point that many of our associates didn't know what it meant. For this reason, Guy reintroduced the Flying Dutchman to a new generation of In-N-Out associates in a special edition of our in-house communication system, BTV, in 1998.

Today we still proudly sell the Flying Dutchman, and our associates all know what it is. Like my dad, I love racing. When it came time to choose my own racing name, I chose Flying Dutch Fox in honor of my own Dutch heritage and in tribute to my father's legacy as the Flying Dutchman—both as a racer and as a leader for In-N-Out Burger.

When Guy Met Lynda

When my dad began as vice president, In-N-Out apparel had been around for a while. But he took our T-shirts to the next level. Soon after the fire, he visited one of the silk screen companies, where he met a graphic artist and salesperson named Lynda Lou Wilson. She was a hardworking single mother of two young daughters.

"So, how come you have a cartoon character on your T-shirts?" Lynda asked. "I thought In-N-Out Burger was more about cars. Have you ever considered offering T-shirts that better represent In-N-Out Burger?"

"How about if you come up with a design and show it to me," Guy said.

Over the next few weeks, Lynda presented several designs to Guy. He liked them, but he never bought any of them. Finally Lynda asked, "I keep showing you designs, but you're not buying. Why?"

Guy, a little shy, replied, "Because I kept wanting to connect with you. I like you."

And that, my friends, was how my father invited my mother out on their first date. Guy and Lynda soon fell in love, and they married on Valentine's Day, February 14, 1981.

Lynda's two daughters, Traci and Teri, were fifteen and twelve when my parents married. They both loved my dad—especially Teri, who adored him. Dad was such a sensitive and sweet guy. He had a good sense

Having fun at the In-N-Out Picnic with her sister, Teri.

of humor and loved to make people laugh. He would use the company plane and have the pilots fly his new family on adventures around the country. They'd gone from living paycheck to paycheck to having these new incredible fun adventures.

Soon Dad expanded the T-shirt side of things so Lynda didn't need to come up with all the designs. He held an annual T-shirt design contest. Top artists would submit their work. Today it's an annual tradition. In-N-Out customers buy, wear, and even collect our shirts.

The Tiny Blonde Girl at Headquarters

A year and a half after my parents were married, Lynda gave birth to a little girl, me, born May 5, 1982. When I came along, my sisters, parents, grandmother, and uncle treasured me. My grandmother and I had a special bond from the start. My family was often at her house, joining her on trips, and going to the In-N-Out Burger offices together. I loved to be with her, visiting friends and family.

As a child I felt valued and cherished by both parents. Some of my favorite earliest memories are when my dad would tuck me into bed at night with a talk, prayer, and a little kiss. Or he'd get me a new toy just to see the delighted look on my face. Dad was also very affectionate with my mom. Another thing he loved to do was make mix tapes for people. He had a microphone in his garage, and he really enjoyed sharing music with his friends and family.

Lynsi with her mother, sister, and grandmother.

When I was little, I had no clue what our family did for a living. But we always had In-N-Out Burger spread in our refrigerator and used it every time my dad cooked burgers on the grill. We also used the spread on BLTs (hold the tomatoes for mine). Friendly faces from In-N-Out Burger visited our home often, but isn't that what friends and family do?

Four Fun Facts About In-N-Out Burger's Spread

1. **An original recipe.** The secret recipe for the spread that we put on our burgers hasn't changed since 1948. It has always been "a spread similar to a Thousand Island dressing," although it's not identical and it's way better. It's designed to be the perfect complement to both the flavor of the toasted bun and the cooked meat patty.

2. **Never "salad dressing" or "sauce."** Associates are taught to use the word "spread" in communication by utilizing the following phrase: "Dressing comes on salad. Sauce comes on spaghetti. We use spread."

3. **Super important to the In-N-Out legacy.** Spread is the first of just two product items specifically mentioned in our four cornerstones: "Our spread recipe will be kept confidential, and our buns will never contain any preservatives."

4. **Mixed with a what?!** Harry originally mixed the spread by hand in a large barrel using a wooden ax handle.

Many of my early childhood experiences revolved around In-N-Out. I sometimes attended the annual In-N-Out Halloween costume parties where my parents dressed up in full costume, enjoying themselves. Our family went with dad to Hawaii, where we joined high-achieving In-N-Out managers. Each year I loved going to the In-N-Out Kids' Christmas party, held in the new warehouse, where they even trucked in enough snow for sledding and I got to play in real snow. All the kids I knew in Southern California went nuts over snow, and this tradition continues today, although it's now held in a bigger venue. In-N-Out was the focus of so many special family times when I was little. I didn't realize until later that the common thread was the family business.

Attending her first In-N-Out Burger Company
Picnic with her uncle, Rich Snyder.

A year before I was born, the company opened the brand-new In-N-Out headquarters and warehouse on several acres in Baldwin Park. I considered the Spanish mission–style revival building to be a mansion. And I wasn't far off. The fifteen-thousand-square-foot building was spacious and elegant. Designed by famed architect Margaret Courtney expressly for In-N-Out, it was chosen as one of the most beautiful buildings in Southern California by Los Angeles Beautiful, an organization that promoted the beautification of the city.[5]

Margaret went on to design twenty-eight restaurants for In-N-Out, along with private residences for my grandmother, uncle, and father. She would later design the buildings of In-N-Out Burger University.

The Original Sign

The first sign for In-N-Out was the iconic sign from the original Store Number 1, which opened October 22, 1948.

IN-N-OUT HAMBURGERS: NO DELAY

An identical sign was used at the second store.

Beginning with the third store, Harry shortened the name of the company to In-N-Out Burger. In 1954, the first property was demolished to make room for the new Interstate 10 freeway. Having lived through two world wars and the Great Depression, Harry knew the value of saving items that still had worth. With his frugality and practicality, he saved what he could from the original Number 1; this included the No Delay sign. When he built the first true warehouse in 1973, he installed the sign near the entrance. Both the truck and the sign survived the 1978 warehouse fire, and both are still operating today!

Although the warehouse has undergone several expansions and a few face-lifts, one thing has remained the same: the original sign for In-N-Out stands near the entrance, and "In-N-Out Hamburgers" still lights up in neon green letters every night. Call it art, call it architecture, or call it just a piece of equipment, this No Delay sign is the oldest existing item belonging to In-N-Out and is the only item to stand witness to the entire history of the company from day one!

At the Baldwin Park company headquarters, a grand fountain out front splashed water into a pool. Every time I visited the new headquarters, either Dad, my grandmother, or Uncle Rich would hand me a coin to toss in so I could make a wish. The fountain was surrounded by terra-cotta tiles imported from Mexico, which paved the walk and extended into the mansion itself. Dad pointed out footprints that coyotes had left in the tiles as they'd dried.

Once we stepped through the enormous carved wooden door into the foyer, I'd gaze up at an imposing oil painting of my grandfather, then look farther up—way up—to the lighted, stained-glass dome in the ceiling. My dad held my hand to guide me up the sweeping, hand-carved staircase that rivaled the one in *Gone with the Wind*. I imagined we were embarking on an adventure. Friendly faces greeted us—plus some imaginary ones.

In Dad's office a stuffed mongoose and cobra stood frozen at the foot of his desk. Dad loved the story "Rikki-Tikki-Tavi" by Rudyard Kipling, rooting as he always did for the underdog. That stuffed mongoose and cobra were real in my mind, so I'd drop to the floor to scold that sneaky snake and encourage the brave mongoose who cleverly protected his family.

Next I'd run off to visit my uncle down the hall. Rich never had any children of his own, and I was his only niece. A devoted uncle, he poured his creativity into my big imagination. I called him "Uncle Riche" (pronounced like "Richie" but spelled with just an *e*), and I remember him as a joy-ful, jolly guy. He kept a raccoon puppet just for my visits, and whenever I walked in, the little puppet would come out to talk to me. I loved it. He cherished every picture I drew or colored for him, and any time I gave him one, he'd immediately have me sign and date it. He saved everything I ever gave him. My dad was the same way with my pictures, and I felt very loved.

Rich's office showed his big personality. It held mementos from his many adventures, including a vintage 1944 Wurlitzer jukebox stocked with old 45s. He let me play songs on it. I was mesmerized watching the record drop and play. Our favorite song was "My Girl," and I loved Otis Redding, Elvis, and anything Motown.

There were framed photos of Uncle Rich with important-looking people, and shelves upon shelves of books. Rich was a big reader. To reach the highest shelves, he had a ladder installed that slid along brass rails. He would let me climb it, then spot me as I explored the treasures way up high, like the mounted bison head from his hunting trip in Montana and a great big moose head. I'd chitchat with those creatures, then scramble down the ladder and head downstairs for my next visit.

I always saved the best for last. My grandmother kept a comfortable office upstairs with Dad and Uncle Rich, but she rarely used it. She pre-ferred to be downstairs with her "girls," as she called them, the women in the accounting department. Grams and the accounting team would greet me and let me play at their desks to my heart's content.

Playing office was one of my favorite games. I loved the calculators, staplers, and ballpoint pens. I still do today. There's just something about office supplies that gives me joy. Grams and her team were always happy to share. Everyone at In-N-Out made me feel so special.

Playing pretend, climbing the ladder in Uncle Rich's office, and "help-ing" or distracting in the accounting office—that's what In-N-Out meant to me as a kid. It was a place I felt at home and loved. I think the people working there enjoyed my visits too. Many of them are still with us today, decades later. We like to celebrate their anniversaries—thirty, forty, even fifty years with In-N-Out Burger. When we do, we always reminisce.

Esther Snyder with her son Rich and President Ronald Reagan.

Sometimes they talk about those visits from a tiny blonde girl with a big imagination. So many have watched me grow up at In-N-Out. I've come alongside them, serving in the stores and in almost every one of In-N-Out's departments. Being able to share pictures together is something I never take for granted. I feel like they're family, and I think the feeling is mutual. I love those memories.

Driving with Dad

I remember Dad's amazing AC Cobra. He liked to work on it, and we were together in his garage one evening when I was a little girl. He lifted me up and set me on the workbench, even though he had limited movement in his right arm from his accident.

On the wall next to the tools and things, he hung up pictures I'd drawn—those endless circles little kids do with crayons. Some drawings were displayed on the door. Showcasing those silly little drawings in his garage showed me he was proud of me.

I looked around on the bench. He kept his work area super organized. Tiny drawers held plastic containers for nuts, bolts, screws, and fuses. While he was working on that engine, Dad let me pull all this stuff out and "organize" it, moving the drawers around and taking things out to play with. I can't imagine I was actually helpful. But he let me play because he enjoyed my company.

When he was finished for the evening, he strapped me into the seat next to him in the Cobra. We drove out of our neighborhood and went for a drive to test how his car was running. I can still hear the comforting rumble of the engine. He drove fast, but I wasn't afraid. Being in that car with him felt magical.

He loved music, too, and we used to talk about the songs we heard on tape and what they meant. Even when I was little, he spoke to me like I was an adult. He never dumbed things down. Somehow he had wisdom and discernment to see that I was going to be exposed to many different things in life. I would need his honest and straightforward approach.

It was dark outside when we returned to the house. I might have fallen asleep. I don't quite remember if he carried me inside. What I do recall from that drive is that for a while, all seemed right with the world. Those first few years of my childhood seemed so perfect, so safe.

I just wish it all had stayed that way.

Chapter Six

OPEN DOORS AND LOTS OF GROWTH

"Behold, I stand at the door and knock. If anyone hears My voice and opens the door, I will come in to him and dine with him, and he with Me."

REVELATION 3:20

BEFORE MY PARENTS MARRIED, MY MOTHER HAD A STRICT "NO DRUGS" policy for anyone she dated. She admits now that she was naive about drugs and didn't know what to look for. My dad had told her about his motorcycle accident and his chronic pain. He'd had a lot of surgeries on his arm, and about 50 percent mobility was restored, but his pain was always there.

Once, when they were dating, she thought she smelled marijuana on him. She confronted him about it. "You need to know that if you can't give that up," she said, "you have to give me up. I'm not going to have that around me or my girls."[1]

Dad promised he would change. They got married and moved to a big house in Glendora, near the San Gabriel mountains. Dad stayed busy with his responsibilities at In-N-Out with the warehouse and meat department. He loved drag racing on weekends and always drove a cool car to and from work. By all outward appearances, they were the perfect young Los Angeles couple.

A few times, my mom says, his behavior turned a bit strange and she thought he might have been drinking. She wasn't aware of his continuing drug issue until she was pregnant with me. One day a friend of Dad's came over to drop off some paperwork. Outside in the yard, the friend handed Dad a folder, then slipped a little bag into my dad's palm, which Dad stuck up his shirtsleeve. My mother saw it all through a window. When Dad came inside, she asked him about the bag. He was honest. Yes, it was marijuana again, which was illegal at the time. He said it eased his pain.

She recommended they ask the doctor for a stronger prescription, something legal. I'm not sure what they gave him that time, but later I found out he used a variety of opiates. I also learned that somewhere along the line he was prescribed hydrocodone, commonly sold as Vicodin.[2]

One day when I was five or six, I couldn't find Dad. He just wasn't around. Mom told me Dad was sick. She took me to visit him in the hospital. The walls, floors, windows, and beds looked like any old hospital to me. I don't remember if someone told me the news or if I eventually figured it out on my own, but this hospital was actually a rehab clinic. At home Dad always kept his drug addiction quiet, and he was highly functional. That was part of the problem.

The Brothers' Dynamic

Tension often swam below the surface between Uncle Rich and Dad. When you're leading a company, you need to walk the fine line between being in charge and trying to control everything. Rich sometimes took a cue from my grandfather and leaned toward micromanaging. On his best days, Dad didn't like taking orders from anyone, much less his little brother. I didn't grasp the full dynamic between my uncle and my dad. I didn't know how much Rich knew about Dad's struggles with pain medications and drugs. But I knew the relationship always required hard work, just as the In-N-Out job did.

Rich was on a success track in business, thanks to the new structure Harry had implemented before he died. My grandfather had appointed Bob

My grandpa's unique two-way speaker box enabled guests to order and receive their meals without leaving their cars. His revolutionary concept introduced California to its first drive-thru hamburger stand.

Early In-N-Out

Throughout our history, we've been blessed with great associates. It has been our associates who have made our success possible, and without their dedication and hard work, In-N-Out Burger would not be the strong company it is today. As we say, "We all work under the same arrow."

Three In-N-Out Burger legends who transformed the company with their leadership, integrity, and service: Phil West, my uncle Rich, and Bob Williams. They hold a special place in my heart for who they were, and for their lasting difference at In-N-Out Burger.

Our commitment to quality starts with our hamburgers. To this day, every burger is made one at a time, cooked fresh to order.

Quality
Cleanliness
Service

For special occasions ... call 338-0087

Our first cookout event was in 1974 with a grill loaded onto a pickup truck. Today, 20 trucks and over 125 associates bring the In-N-Out experience to picnics, schools, churches, birthdays, and weddings.

Two of In-N-Out's greatest leaders: my father (right) and my uncle Rich (left). They were special men.

The Snyder Brothers

Uncle Rich was a one-of-a-kind uncle and leader. Of my family members, I was closest to him—other than my parents—and we had a special bond. I'll never forget the times we had and the memories we made.

My grandpa was an incredibly hard worker who had an unwavering commitment to quality. He set and maintained high standards, and he believed in cleanliness, quality, and service. I've promised to keep my grandparents' memory and legacy alive, always.

Grams sure was an amazing woman. Her spirit of generosity still drives us, and In-N-Out Burger wouldn't be what it is today without her heart and hard work.

My Grams and Grandpa made each burger by hand with love. Although times have changed, our mission of quality, cleanliness, and friendliness has stayed the same.

My dad with my brother-in-law and former In-N-Out Burger chief operating officer, Mark Taylor. He is a great friend and a pool of wisdom for me to draw from.

Great times with my dad, mom, and sisters. I will never forget the days we spent together.

We've always been a family of car lovers, which dates back to my grandpa's part ownership in the historic Irwindale Raceway. He sold burgers that were basically unbranded In-N-Out burgers in the concession stands to racers and fans.

In-N-Out Racing

Debuting my Top Sportsman '69 Chevelle at the 2023 NHRA Winternationals. It was an awesome moment since it was the first event at the newly renamed In-N-Out Burger Pomona Dragstrip.

My dad and I at the dragstrip. He had a lifelong interest in cars and drag racing, and we shared so many memories around music in cool cars or trucks.

The In-N-Out Burger–sponsored Top Fuel Dragster in 1998.

The In-N-Out Burger Nitro Funny Car. Our family sponsored Funny Cars for a season.

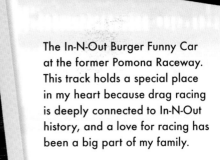

The In-N-Out Burger Funny Car at the former Pomona Raceway. This track holds a special place in my heart because drag racing is deeply connected to In-N-Out history, and a love for racing has been a big part of my family.

My best friend, who has made a musician out of me, as I've brought back the musician in him.

In-N-Out Today

Sean and I representing our In-N-Out Burger Ugly Christmas Sweaters.

Our executive leadership team members are all so special and integral to our success as a company. I work with the best people and love this family so much.

One of my favorite things to do with some of my favorite people is playing company events with the In-N-Out Burger company band, .48 Special.

It's always exciting to welcome a new store to our In-N-Out family. Behind every store opening are hours of hard work by our leaders and associates in order to serve our customers "Quality You Can Taste."

We love celebrating our amazing and hardworking associates at family Picnics. One of my favorite things to do is play with the band and look out to see our In-N-Out family and their friends having a good time.

Quality will always be the most important ingredient at In-N-Out Burger.

Brothers Guy and Rich Snyder at the opening
for Store Number 64 in 1990.

Williams to help oversee the company.* He had decades of experience and
had been personally trained by Harry. After Harry's passing, Rich promoted
Bob Lang Sr. and Chuck Papez to be divisional managers, each with nine
stores. Rich fully embraced this structure, and he was a hard charger. By the
time I was born in May 1982, Rich had grown the company from eighteen
to twenty-five stores. Right before my fifth birthday, the count was up to
forty-five.

I loved Rich, who always treated me like his daughter. My dad never
had a problem with that. They both adored me and, having endured so
much pain in their own young years, they wanted me to have a childhood
that was pure, fun, and loving.

---

* Bob Williams was the general manager over Chuck Papez and Bob Lang Sr. Stores were overseen by
Bob and the divisional managers, who had nine stores each (eighteen total stores).

Rich Snyder with Lynsi enjoying time together
at Guy and Lynda Snyder's ranch.

Rich celebrated birthdays and holidays with our family, and sometimes
he'd take me on special trips, like when we took my grandmother to visit her
childhood home in Illinois. I think my uncle and my dad did all the things
for me that they wished they could have had in their childhood. My toys
were never taken away in punishment. Each Christmas a pile of wrapped
presents sat under our tree, all marked for me. A few extra unwrapped ones
were supposed to be from Santa. Besides all that, there was always one big
gift. (I remember an exciting pedal car.) When I grew old enough to begin
wondering if Santa was actually real, Rich and my parents were jokingly
horrified. They hired someone to dress up in a red suit and beard and climb
up onto our roof. I also caught Santa in my living room one year. I was
convinced!

My uncle always valued what I said, even when I was very young. He
asked me a lot of questions about In-N-Out, just to get my feelings on
things. When I was only five he asked me things like, "How many stores
should we open, Lynsi?" If I told him ten, he'd make it his goal to open ten
stores the next year, or at least that's what he conveyed to me. I'm sure his
plans were more complex than that, but the treasure left in my mind was
that he listened to me. He wanted me to weigh in on things that mattered

to him. He assured me that my young voice carried clout in his life, in the family business, and even with customers. That was a tremendous gift.

When I was ten, Rich had In-N-Out business cards made for me that read, "Lynsi Snyder, Children's Affairs." I was delighted that my opinion mattered so much. Both my dad and my uncle were lavishly supportive of me. Perhaps because they didn't feel valued by their dad, they gave me all that they wished they'd received from him. They always listened, took me seriously, and genuinely cared about what I said.

I recognize that the way I was raised was also part of God's plan for my life. I don't believe in coincidences; and besides, God knew my future. He knew what kind of upbringing I would need to handle the years ahead. Rich and Dad instilled in me the confidence to believe that what I said mattered even when they weren't around to say so. They would believe in me even when others didn't.

Playing with her father, Guy Snyder, during Christmas.

An Organized and Fun Approach

Uncle Riche loved everything about Disney. I can't count the number of times he took me to Disneyland. It was one of our favorite fun places to go together, and sometimes he picked up business ideas there. Rich learned that Walt Disney had designed staff name tags at Disneyland to resemble miniature welcome signs. That inspired Rich to have similar name tags made for In-N-Out, engraved with associates' names. It communicated a sense of welcome to customers. With our names clearly visible, customers could greet us by name, if they chose. We've always enjoyed getting to know our guests.

Learning about Walt Disney and other creative businesspeople fueled Rich's ambitions. Even though Rich was young as a CEO, he wanted to grow as a leader. He took every opportunity to become the best possible steward of In-N-Out. Rich read business books on leadership and growth. He joined the international network known as the Young Presidents' Organization, where other young leaders (ages forty-five and younger) gathered to discuss business ideas, trends, and research. This group invigorated Rich, and he shared what he was learning with the rest of our team.

My grandfather had always honored customers, and Rich picked up that trend and took it to the next level. He developed the In-N-Out motto, "The Customer Is Everything to Us," and had it imprinted on company stationery. To this day, each piece of communication that goes out from our headquarters proudly proclaims, "God Bless America. The Customer Is Everything to Us."

Rich established what he called our Golden Rule. It came in two parts. Rule number one: The customer is always right. Rule number two: If by chance the customer is wrong, refer back to rule number one. To Uncle Rich, it was all very simple. When our customers pull up to In-N-Out, we want them to feel like they're in a safe haven. They're welcomed, never second-guessed, and we genuinely want to see them and serve them.

History of the In-N-Out Burger Tire Gauge

A customer at In-N-Out Burger Store Number 61 in Vista once asked the manager if he or any of the associates had a tire pressure gauge to test the pressure in his car's tires. After checking, the manager replied that, unfortunately, neither he nor his associates had a tire gauge for the customer.

The manager at the time was Kelly King, and he cared greatly about our customers. In this instance, Kelly felt he had failed to fulfill the customer's need. The incident moved him to immediately purchase a tire gauge, which he kept in his shirt pocket from then on. The move was Kelly's way of showing that a customer would never again have to worry about getting their tire pressure checked.

More than that, if Kelly could help it, no customers would have any of their requests unmet. Keeping a tire pressure gauge in his pocket served as a reminder that the customer is our most important asset. Our job is taking care of them.

Kelly's reaction to this incident serves as an example of how we at In-N-Out feel when we do not meet customers' expectations or needs. We're moved to do something about it. To the best of our abilities we actively look for solutions. What's unique about this situation is that the customer's request was a bit unusual. But that did not stop Kelly from doing what he was supposed to do—serve our customers.

Rich also established what he called the Four Nevers to help resolve issues and give customers the best possible In-N-Out experience:

1. Never give excuses.
2. Never argue with the customer.
3. Never put the customer on the defensive.
4. Never make a big deal of a complaint.

"After all," he would say, "the particulars of a disagreement don't matter." We still use Rich's Four Nevers as part of our training. In ultimate terms, our customers sign our paychecks. The Four Nevers ensure that our customers experience the consistent respect they deserve. We want them to know they're our biggest asset. In fact, printed under the signature line on every check we issue, it says, "This check was made possible by the customer."

Rich created the In-N-Out Mission / Purpose Statement in the 1980s. Essentially, he formalized what Harry and Esther had been doing for decades. To this day many of our associates know our Mission / Purpose Statement by heart.

You may have noticed that my uncle Rich was a fan of lists and statements. Good thing too! His organized mind gave us gems we still use today—not only our mission statement but what we call the Four Cornerstones (and even more, which you'll find in the Insider Info).

Breakfast with the Boss

Rich had seen firsthand from my grandparents some of the good ways family and business could intertwine. He built on their principles when he began inviting associates who aimed for management over for breakfast at his house. Rich shared business and leadership ideas, and the gatherings provided a discussion forum that helped shape Rich's budding leadership style. Meanwhile, using Harry's tried-and-true methods, Jack Ruley continued to teach the management trainees at Store Number 1.

In 1984, Rich launched the In-N-Out University training center on the very spot where my grandparents' Baldwin Park home once stood in the late 1940s and 1950s. At the start, the university housed one classroom and a working kitchen to serve lunch Monday through Friday to students, associates, and the public. It eventually became the hub for learning about the company. Today it's where we coach all levels of management, equip teams, and develop and teach our training materials. It's a vibrant, beautiful school where we share our company's dynamic history and culture. Our current building was constructed here in 2005. We also have training centers in Lathrop, California; Lancaster, Texas; Phoenix, Arizona; and soon in Colorado Springs, Colorado.

Just like Harry, Rich hoped that ambitious associates would make a career of working with In-N-Out. As a motivated visionary, he started career development programs where In-N-Out paid for associates' continuing education—including tuition and books at our university. This fit with Harry and Esther's philosophy of encouraging the associates' ambitions and dreams.

On June 17, 1988, Rich met a milestone. He opened our fiftieth store, located at 72265 Varner Road in Thousand Palms, California. A year later, he opened our Company Store at In-N-Out's original Baldwin Park location, where customers could purchase everything from In-N-Out socks to In-N-Out beach chairs. A great selection of T-shirts was always available. Today you'll find the In-N-Out Company Store at three locations—the original in Baldwin Park and two in Las Vegas—plus an online store.

Beginning in 1989, Rich tweaked our store layouts. For Store Number 56 in Barstow, he installed three grills—another first—to accommodate increasing store traffic. In 1990, he opened Store Number 64 in West Covina, California, on I-10, which features a split-level dining area. This restaurant served as a research and development launching ground for new equipment and customer service innovations. Mark Taylor became that store's manager, and it was one of our busiest stores. Mark also happens to be the husband of my oldest sister, Traci.

Mark and Traci met in high school. When Harry learned that Mark was on the management track at a competitor's restaurant, he invited Mark to come to In-N-Out for an interview. Mark was hired, starting as an hourly associate. He worked his way up to store manager, then opened Number 64, a key location for the company. In coming years Mark would be appointed to the role of divisional manager, general manager, vice president of operations, and eventually president and chief operating officer of In-N-Out Burger.

Ambitious Goals

Rich worked hard to care for store managers, encouraging each to think of his or her store as their own. He inspired them to dream big and achieve lofty goals, and he continued the trend of paying them well.

Additionally, Rich provided strong incentives, like the perks of what we today call our Club 1095 trips. Historically, Harry and Esther began the trend. They invited Chuck Papez and his wife, Barbara, to Hawaii when Chuck's store became the highest volume store in those early days. Other managers were rewarded with a variety of trips, depending on how well their stores performed. But under Harry, managers of lower-volume stores could only earn less pricey trips, maybe Reno or Vegas. Only managers of high-volume stores could earn Hawaii.

Rich leveled the field so each store competes only against itself, regardless of volume.[†] He set up an incentive program so any manager who achieves 95 percent of his or her goals over three years would win a top-rated trip. Goals could be about a higher burger volume, or labor, safety, or mystery shopper scores. Since the time frame to reach the goals was three years, or 1,095 days, they dubbed the incentive Club 1095. The name suggests another twist. If a store manager achieves 95 percent of goals over a three-year period, then the manager is a "10"—thus, 1095!

---

† Rich made this decision in consultation with Ed Pendleton (1967–2016, retired as divisional manager), Wendell Ansnes (1971–2021, retired as QFC and divisional manager), Greg Fairchild (1972–2019 retired as divisional manager), and Gary Murphy (1971–2021).

By the end of 1991, after Rich had run the company for fourteen years, In-N-Out had seventy-one stores. That year he cast a giant vision. By the year 2000, he wanted In-N-Out to have two hundred stores. Such an ambitious goal demanded innovation. That's when we developed the Strategic Planning Initiative. He wanted great people on board for each new store we opened.

As part of the initiative, for the first time in In-N-Out's history, Rich called for a completely fresh set of eyes on the company. He had struck up a friendship with Carl Van Fleet, an executive with Rusty Pelican Restaurants, and he knew that Carl also loved In-N-Out. Rich took his time with the hire. Carl had seven interviews. He even had to meet with a psychiatrist. Ultimately Carl was hired as the vice president of quality, friendliness, and cleanliness (QFC). In the years to come, Carl played an important role in creating and managing our QFC operation, providing feedback and setting goals while helping maintain our high standards and consistency.

Along with the new outside hire, Rich began what he called the All-Star Program, designed to help the company expand in ways that worked. Rich knew that opening a new In-N-Out Burger store is an intense experience. Our standard is perfection, even if the line is a hundred cars long—not uncommon for the first few days of a new store. Under the program, about fifteen All-Star associates form a team to coordinate the opening of each new store. They help with cleaning, supplying, hiring, and training. They're all there when the doors open and the lights go on. Then, when the new associates get up to speed, the All-Stars gradually peel off, return to their home stores, and leave the new store in the capable hands of the local team.

Today we have much larger All-Star teams. They're specialists who make a premium wage and aren't afraid of working long hours. An All-Star must be experienced, with proven skills to ensure the smoothest operations. This guarantees that when a new store opens, customers enjoy a flawless experience right from the get-go. The All-Star teams are awesome and pave the way into new markets for us, showing locals the In-N-Out way.

Rich mused about how customers could reach us easily, ask questions, raise concerns, or just tell us about their In-N-Out experience. He worked with In-N-Out executive Carl Van Fleet to establish our 800 line, a direct, toll-free phone line available every day from the time the first store's door opens until the last door closes. They trained a team of associates with in-store experience to take care of each customer who calls. It was important to Rich that customers speak to someone in person, not just leave a message. He wanted to hear both good and bad. It's worth noting that our most frequent calls are requests about adding locations, directions to the nearest stores, how to apply for a job, and how to book a cookout. Today Eric Billings leads this department of more than eighty associates.[‡]

To make the most of every moment on the job, Rich enlisted a customized bus, built like a rolling office. Rather than just sit in a fixed office and ask vendors, customers, and associates to come to him, he decided he'd take all his meetings on the road, stopping to visit stores along the way. It was a savvy move—Rich was regularly able to meet in person with key associates and vendors. It even set up an image that this was a company going places.

Rich was a wellspring of ideas. He came up with the idea of Burger Television (BTV), a media outlet where we could virtually draw all company associates together, keep everyone informed, and support training and development so we could continue to provide excellence in quality, friendliness, and cleanliness to better serve the customer. That has been the goal from day one, and it's the top priority for our team today.

Rich asked his colleague Jack Sims to assemble a production team to create BTV content. Jack secured several people to film and edit each show. He asked film editor Bill Scherer to lead one of the edit sessions. Bill recalls, "I was a young guy with several clients and solid industry experience with television and film production, music creation, writing and post-production editing and effects. We worked well together and took a great liking to one another. Rich and Jack asked me to take on editing the show moving forward. As time went on, I was asked to take on larger roles in the creation process of BTV. Rich produced regular content for the show, delivering messages to the associates, and encouraging everyone to do all they could

---

[‡] We invite customers to contact us with any issue or to ask any questions about the company at 1-800-786-1000.

to care for the customer."[3] BTV is shown at store meetings, which happen every four weeks. To this day, Bill is still part of the In-N-Out family. We've worked together for a couple of decades.

The Snyder Brothers

As the years progressed, Rich did much good for the company, yet his relationship with his brother remained complicated. They loved each other—they even went on vacations together—but they butted heads a lot. Guy was the older brother, but Rich was at the helm of the business. Sometimes my dad has been portrayed as the more rebellious brother in the family, while Rich is seen as the golden boy who could do no wrong. But that's not entirely accurate. My dad had a lot of good to him, and although Rich did a lot of good, he also struggled with several issues including occasional cocaine use and an addiction to diet pills in the 1980s, which I found out about only when I was older. Both my father and my uncle were big, tall men, and they were both "gentle giants" in personality type and demeanor. Yet they both had their fierce sides and could both be highly competitive, which added to the tension between them. It was a complicated relationship.

My dad decided to create space between them. In 1989, when I was seven, we moved to a 167-acre ranch he bought, which was approximately six hundred miles north in Shingletown, California, an eight-hour drive from In-N-Out headquarters in Baldwin Park. Personally, I loved living in Shingletown. I became involved in 4-H and took care of pygmy goats. Through 4-H I started to do public speaking, which helped me later in life. I loved my school, and I got pretty good grades. It felt like nobody knew that our family was connected to a business, and I liked that sense of anonymity as a child.

Dad loved it too. Up at the ranch, away from the busyness of Los Angeles, he could be a family man. In those early years he and I often played outside together or watched movies or played video games. I remember having a birthday party with a bunch of friends, and he rented a cotton candy machine for us. He had an old surplus army tank, and at my birthday parties he'd drive all my friends around in his tank just for fun. They loved it. It was so important to my dad to see his family enjoying life. His dad had been a workaholic and hadn't given much time to his boys when they were young, so my father really wanted to do it right. He went out of his way to spend time with me.

According to those who knew him well at the time, he did better there than he'd done in a long time. Here's how my mom puts it:

> Guy just could not find happiness in the corporate world. He didn't want to be there. He was the type of guy who just wanted to be free. He was happy to get up every morning and go out at the crack of dawn and ride the tractor, enjoying life on the mountain. There were lakes and trails all over the ranch, and he was building new trails with the tractor—he was so happy.[4]

A few good years passed. As Uncle Riche neared his fortieth birthday, he began dating a woman fourteen years younger than him. Guy thought the age gap was too great, and the arguing between the brothers seemed to intensify. Rich tried to buy out my dad's shares and his inheritance in the family company. That attempt hurt my father and caused further tension in their relationship. Rich married his girlfriend on May 2, 1992, in Maui. Notably, my mom and dad didn't attend the wedding.

Rich and his new bride settled into home life, moving to Newport Beach and buying a smaller house for my grandmother. My uncle looked happy. Rich enjoyed his hot air balloon and his sailboat. He threw block parties for his new neighbors. He liked to laugh. He and his new wife planned to have children soon. Everything was coming together for Rich.

But huge heartache lay right around the corner.

Chapter Seven

THE WORST NIGHT
OF OUR LIVES

Surely He has borne our griefs
And carried our sorrows.

ISAIAH 53:4

FOR A WHILE, RICH CONTINUED HIS UPWARD TRAJECTORY WITH THE company. He made a point to bring fun and joy to the job in a way only he could. For instance, Uncle Rich loved our annual kids' Christmas parties, which rose to new levels in the 1980s, the era when Rich led the company. Every store carried Christmas in the air, and the festive atmosphere encouraged by Rich spread to everyone who worked for In-N-Out.

I love the story about associate Jon Peterson, who was driving by Store Number 1 on the way to get his Christmas tree with his family. His son, about five years old, saw the In-N-Out sign and announced he was hungry. Jon pulled over. He and his son went to the walk-up window while his wife stayed in the car. As they waited in line, our butcher came out of the back room dressed like Santa Claus from head to foot. He nodded warmly at the boy, and said to the father, "Hi Jon, how are you doing?"

The little boy gasped. They got their food and returned to their car. "Mom, you'll never guess what," the boy said. "We saw Santa Claus, and he knew us!"[1]

It didn't need to be Christmas for Rich to stir up fun. As stores were

On the first day of CHRISTMAS, my true love sent to me. On the second day of CHRISTMAS, my true love sent to me. On the third day of CHRISTMAS, my true love sent to me. On the fourth day of CHRISTMAS, my true love sent to me. On the fifth day of CHRISTMAS, my true love sent to me. On the sixth day of CHRISTMAS, my true love sent to me. On the seventh day of CHRISTMAS, my true love sent to me. On the eighth day of CHRISTMAS, my true love sent to me. On the ninth day of CHRISTMAS, my true love sent to me. On the tenth day of CHRISTMAS, my true love sent to me. On the eleventh day of CHRISTMAS, my true love sent to me. On the twelfth day of CHRISTMAS, my true love sent to me.

The In-N-Out Burger Christmas card from 2008.

added, managers and divisional managers began gathering outside of work, on their own initiative. They enjoyed being together, and Rich took notice. In the early 1980s, In-N-Out manager Ed Pendleton went to a picnic held by Boyd's Market Grocery, where his wife, Diane, worked. They had a great time, and the next day Ed suggested to Rich that they ought to organize similar picnics for In-N-Out. Rich attended one of the Boyd's picnics to see for himself. There, he turned to Ed and said, "We can do this."[2]

That's how a beloved In-N-Out tradition was born. Each year the entire company attends a picnic. On the first day half the company picnics with their families while the other half works, then vice versa. In the early days, divisional and store managers and their spouses staffed the picnics. Today the picnics are attended by thousands and staffed primarily by associates.

Guy Snyder (left) enjoying an In-N-Out Company Picnic
with Vice President Bob Williams (center).

Bob Lang Sr. recalls, "It was fun watching the kids growing up, getting to see each other's families through the years. In-N-Out is one giant family."[3]

I have so many good memories of our In-N-Out family picnics. Uncle Rich and my dad knew how to have fun. We played volleyball, ate burgers, and, yes, even had hot dogs. Once, Uncle Rich rented a real live elephant to give rides to us kids. Associate Jon Peterson created a big In-N-Out banner that said something like "Free elephant rides here." But instead of an elephant, the contractor, huffing and puffing, brought over a camel.

"What do I want with a camel?" Uncle Rich said.

"Well, the elephant was busy," the contractor said with a shrug. Everybody got a big laugh out of that, and the kids had massive fun riding the camel.[4] The next year, the elephant arrived and became a regular attraction for several years. I remember riding it when I was young.

Our company has grown to the point where we hold nine picnics each

At a regional In-N-Out picnic.

summer: Southern California, Northern California, Oregon, Las Vegas, Arizona, Utah, Colorado, Dallas–Fort Worth, and Austin–San Antonio–Houston. Our amazing In-N-Out events team plans them. We want to keep the fun rolling. We hold contests and games, award prizes, and always stage entertainment. (For more on the culture of fun competition we've built at In-N-Out, see the Insider Info #3: Friendly Competition.) When I see our hardworking associates having fun, every second of work we've put into these events feels worth it.

Tucking In Faith Reminders

Before we go any further, I need to emphasize what Uncle Riche saw as his legacy of faith in the company he worked so hard for. I know it was important to him, and I love how it's grown. Customers often notice Bible verses printed on In-N-Out products, and that practice has a history tied to my good memories about Uncle Rich.

Both Dad and Uncle Rich grew up with some faith in their home. As boys, my grandmother told them about God and taught them how to pray. When they were teens and young men, they wandered from their faith. But in the early 1980s, Rich reconnected with God in a much bigger way. He became an active member of Costa Mesa's Calvary Chapel, led by Pastor Chuck Smith, and dedicated his life to Jesus. Rich didn't claim to be perfect. But he finally found that the deep need in his heart could only be satisfied by Jesus and by finding his own identity in him. I remember my uncle telling me once, "I'm not always a good Christian, but I'm a Christian."

Around 1987, Rich began printing tiny references to Bible verses on In-N-Out paper goods. It was a way for him to express his faith, and he wanted to put that little touch of faith on our brand. In a 1990 episode of BTV, Rich explained, "I quietly did it a few years ago. I'm a Christian. For those who know me, they definitely know that I'm not perfect and neither is In-N-Out. We are trying to serve our communities and do a good job the best we can. I guess the reason [for the verses] is it's my way of thanking God for helping In-N-Out so much. I took over In-N-Out when I was twenty-four years old, and for me it was kind of tough. I thank God that he helped me."[5]

To this day, Revelation 3:20 is discreetly printed on hamburger and cheeseburger bags. Nahum 1:7 is on the Double-Double wrappers. Proverbs 3:5 sits underneath milkshake cups, Isaiah 9:6 is on Christmas cups, and John 3:16 is underneath soda cups.

That tradition continues to this day. After I became president, I added Proverbs 24:16 to our fry boats, Luke 6:35 to coffee cups, and John 13:34 to the hot cocoa cups. (See each verse listed out in Insider Info #2: Bible Verses on In-N-Out Packaging.) We never try to force our beliefs on anyone, and customers with any faith tradition, or none, are certainly welcome through our doors. We hire and promote associates and managers who don't share our faith. God loves all people, and so do we! My family simply wants our faith to take a meaningful place in everything our company does. The verses act as encouragements. Always, the goal is to love God and to love other people, and we've learned the platform of love is huge.

The feedback we get about the Bible verses is almost always positive. Customers don't always share our faith, but they appreciate that we're honest about our own faith journey and that we want it to be part of the integrity of our company. Many commend our efforts to reach out, care for people, and lead with love.

An awareness of the blessings God has given inspires generosity. I think that was Rich's intention in 1991, when he began sending In-N-Out Cookout Trailers to the missions around Los Angeles to prepare meals for the unhoused. That's how the In-N-Out Feed the Homeless Program began, as a quiet way of providing delicious meals for the less fortunate.

We currently serve people involved with the Los Angeles Mission, Ventura Rescue Mission, San Diego Rescue Mission, and Long Beach Mission. These initiatives fit beautifully with part three of our mission statement, which states our purpose to help "communities in our marketplace [become] stronger, safer, and better places to live." We invite other people to serve alongside us too. It's better to give than to receive.

Welcome to Nevada

Uncle Rich loved a great celebration, and that's how he brought In-N-Out Burger into Nevada. Las Vegas Store Number 80 opened in 1992 on November 17, followed by Store Number 81 the very next day.* Our stores had never moved outside of California before. The huge In-N-Out "state-line party" featured the Flying Elvis (an Elvis impersonator) and lunch on the border of California and Nevada. The party wrapped up with Uncle Rich and a bunch of In-N-Out volunteers roping up for fun and dragging one of our eighteen-wheelers across the state line, just to see if they could move a big rig.

Later, when Store Number 86 opened in Las Vegas at 14888 Dean Martin Drive, we unveiled the largest sign in In-N-Out's history. For years it was the largest restaurant sign anywhere, and Vegas just seemed the place to do things in a really big way. At fifty-five feet wide, the sign featured two miles of neon coiled inside it, so Vegas Strip motorists would be sure to see it.

Next Rich looked north, with plans to open two stores in Fresno, three hours' drive from Baldwin Park. The first Fresno store opened in November 1992, with the second opening less than a month later. The Fresno store openings helped prompt what we considered a watershed change for In-N-Out, switching from Pepsi to Coke.

In many ways, In-N-Out is a nostalgic restaurant. It invokes a simpler time. We've barely changed our menu since we first opened in 1948, and we take our loyalty to longtime customers and vendors very seriously. For years In-N-Out had used Pepsi products, and we believed we had a strong mutual relationship. (This includes a line of collectible glassware, which you can read about in Insider Info #7: Collectibles and Special Items under the heading "History of In-N-Out Glassware.") For years we held an agreement that the two companies wouldn't compete in any way. But PepsiCo slowly began acquiring fast-food restaurants as part of their

---

* The stores were managed by Jaime Marquez and Blande Pittman, respectively.

overall company makeup, which Rich watched closely. PepsiCo acquired Pizza Hut in 1977. The next year, they purchased Taco Bell, and in 1986, they acquired KFC. Rich started to feel like he was buying product from his competitors.

Then in 1990, PepsiCo, under its Taco Bell brand, acquired Hot 'n Now, a restaurant chain that sold burgers and focused on drive-thru service and underselling the competition. At its height, Hot 'n Now had about 150 restaurants in fifteen states, mostly in the Midwest, although they were eyeing the West Coast, zeroing in on California. Rich grew alarmed when he learned that Pepsi had bought a fourth fast-food chain. He communicated with the Pepsi CEO via letter, voicing his concern. They told him, essentially, that they were only testing the markets and promised not to open any restaurants where In-N-Out is located. Shortly afterward, they announced an opening in Fresno. We weren't in Fresno yet, but we would be shortly. It was already planned. A few weeks later they opened a restaurant in Irvine, which wouldn't have been possible if it hadn't already been in the works. We've been serving Coke products ever since.

When Rich and Guy Hugged

In tandem with Rich's growing success, the tension between the two brothers grew and reached a peak in 1993. After Rich's wedding in 1992, the rift between Guy and Rich had widened. Complicating things, Rich seemed determined to buy out my father's share of the company, which Dad didn't want to do. Dad was still working for In-N-Out, but he spent little time at the office. He was doing well in the fight against his addictions, but his pain was relentless.

In December 1993, when I was eleven years old, I hadn't seen Uncle Rich in a while, although he had sent Christmas presents and we talked on the phone. As I thanked him, I had an idea. "Can you come to my Christmas play?" I asked. My parents shot each other a look. Things were tense between them and Rich. When I hung up the phone and told them that Rich had agreed, they both looked surprised. I found out later he asked for permission to attend.

The date arrived, and Uncle Rich flew up to Shingletown to see me in my performance, which I was so excited about. After the show ended, I saw Uncle Riche and Dad talking. That made me happy. Then something happened that flooded me with joy. As I watched, they hugged. I found out later my uncle had asked my dad for forgiveness.

"I don't know, Rich," Dad said. My dad was trying to wrap his mind around forgiveness, but it was all still so painful.

"Guy, I don't know when I'll see you again," Rich said. "I love you."

Without missing a beat, Dad said, "I love you too, Rich."

That night, Rich returned home to Los Angeles. The next morning dawned bright, December 15, 1993. My grandmother and Rich, along with consultant Jack Sims and In-N-Out general manager Bob Williams, flew northward on a small chartered Westwind 24A jet for the opening of our new Store Number 93 in Fresno and to scout for new locations.[6] Friends recall Esther saying that it was a beautiful day in Fresno and that she and Rich had a good time celebrating the store's opening.

Phil West, executive vice president and Rich's closest friend, joined them in Fresno. The pair had known each other since preschool, and Rich relied heavily on Phil. Strangely, they had a long-standing policy never to fly together. They were afraid that if the plane went down, there would be no one to carry on. That day, Phil had booked a ticket back to Los Angeles on a commercial flight, but his plane was delayed. Rich said, "It's Christmas. Why don't you fly with us and get home early."[7] Phil joined the others on the Westwind jet for the return trip. This was the only time they had ever flown together.

Fresno is about 234 miles north of Los Angeles. On the return trip the plane made stops in Bakersfield, about 128 miles from Los Angeles, and La Verne, about twenty minutes east of Baldwin Park, before it was scheduled to land at John Wayne Airport in Santa Ana. In La Verne, my grandmother and Bob Williams deplaned because they both lived closer to that airport.

I will never forget that evening. My parents and I were at the ranch in

Shingletown, and Dad and I were playing the video game *Jurassic Park* on Sega Genesis. I was eleven years old. When the phone rang we paused the game. The action on-screen stayed suspended in that moment. Rick Plate, an In-N-Out executive assistant for the Snyder family, was on the line. Mom took the call, then handed the phone to Dad. I couldn't hear all that was said, but Dad suddenly sobbed then burst out wailing. Mom joined him on the back patio, crying with him. They came inside.

The plane had crashed near John Wayne Airport. We were told there were no survivors.

I couldn't absorb the news. *No way,* my mind protested. *This isn't possible. Maybe it's not Uncle Rich's plane.*

My parents quickly decided to head to Los Angeles to be with everyone there, awaiting further news. We hurried to pack. I remember standing in my closet, dazed, staring at my clothes, wondering what to put in my suit-case. I kept thinking, *Maybe it wasn't Rich's plane. Maybe it's someone else.* I remember walking back through the living room and seeing our video game paused, hovering, still suspended. I knew my life would never be the same again. Though I was a daddy's girl at heart, my closeness with Uncle Riche was the next best thing to the relationship I had with my dad. At just forty-one, he was far too young to die. I was devasted.

As painful as it was for me, I knew it was worse for my dad. He and Rich had such a complicated history. He went outside and cried out his brother's name. I heard his raw pain in that yell. I think my dad was wishing that he had specifically forgiven Rich the night before, that he had just let go of all of it. Rich was the only person in the world who truly understood what my dad had been through. After all they'd endured as children, Rich wasn't only a brother. He was my dad's best friend, despite all their tensions.

At least they'd hugged each other and spoken their mutual love. I can't imagine how painful it would have been if they hadn't had that conver-sation. There was a comfort in that, at least. He was unable to conceive the depths of what had happened. His brother had deeply hurt him and I'm sure he wanted to forgive, but it was so raw. They hadn't spoken in so long, and a quick conversation wasn't enough to completely resolve and forgive each other.

It wasn't easy for us to get onto a plane that evening. When we landed in Los Angeles, we went straight to meet my grandmother and Rich's wife. My parents hugged them both.

Bits and pieces of the news came out that evening and in the days to come. The crash had occurred about 5:30 p.m. as their plane descended into John Wayne Airport.[8] Tragically, the plane had been caught in the wake turbulence of a larger 757 airliner, sending their smaller plane crashing to the ground. The pilot, Stephen Barkin, and copilot, John McDaniel, were killed along with Jack Sims, Phil West, and Uncle Rich.

Gone but Never Forgotten

The story circulated in the news for days. At In-N-Out we worked to carry on, but palpable grief descended over the company.

Keith Brazeau (1973–2018, retired as VP of quality, friendliness, and cleanliness) recalls the events of the night of the crash.

I was working in the Irvine office building when I was approached by Phil West's executive assistant. She had just received a call from Phil's wife, Lori, saying he hadn't returned from the Fresno trip yet. She went on to tell me a plane had crashed some eight miles away. I left the office building and went to the crash site. It was a mess.

I had a license plate with INO on it. I had a windbreaker with the logo, INOBF [In-N-Out Burger Foundation]. Normally, you are excited to show that you work for In-N-Out, but media was already swarming the site, so many cameras and reporters. I grabbed a roll of masking tape that I had in my car, covered my license plate and the jacket logo, then made my way to the fire department command trailer at the crash site. I made contact with Rick Plate, the Snyder family assistant.

Rick had already called Guy at his ranch in Shingletown. Lynda had answered the phone and Rick asked to speak to Guy, but before letting her go, Rick asked for Lynda's help in maintaining Guy's composure because he had some bad news to report. Rick explained the situation to Guy. Guy's first words were, "Get me a plane. I need to be with my INO family."[9]

Donna Turkmani, Rick Plate's wife and a family friend, remembers it this way:

My husband, Rick, was at the airport to meet Rich. I received a call from Rick telling me about the crash. They believed there were no survivors. He asked me to pick up Lori West [wife of Phil] and take her to the home of Chris Snyder [Rich's wife].

The crash site was blocked off and we weren't allowed too close. It was agreed that it was best for the family to stay elsewhere while we awaited further word. Although we knew that it was their plane, we had to wait for official notification and identification. We then moved to the Embassy Suites, where we were given a suite to assemble in. By the time we arrived, Esther, other family members, friends, and associates had already arrived. Together, we waited for news.

Sometime later in the evening, once it became official that it was their plane, more and more people arrived to lend their support, and we moved to Rich's Newport home.

Much of that night is a blur, but I remember that late that night, in typical Snyder fashion, Esther and Guy put their grief aside for a moment and recorded a video message to all their associates reassuring us that we would be okay, and that we would get through this together. Esther was one of the strongest women I know. She put her faith in God, picked herself up, and kept going.

Over the next week, although our world had been turned upside down, family, friends, associates, and vendors rallied together to help organize three separate funerals [held at Calvary Chapel in Costa Mesa]—for Rich, Phil West, and Jack Sims—and a combined memorial service, all the while keeping the daily workings of In-N-Out going. Everyone pulled together, worked through their grief, and did their best. I think we all believed the same thing: If the Snyders could keep going, we could too.[10]

The tragic loss of these beloved In-N-Out executives was felt by all. Bill Scherer, from In-N-Out's BTV, recalls,

Rich and Jack often brought me along on flights to new store openings to cover the event for BTV and to assist Rich with other production interests. It was unusual when Rich and Jack shared that I would stay behind for one of our upcoming openings in Fresno. I think maybe realizing that I was feeling left out, they called me from the store when they arrived and shared their feelings toward me, their appreciation of our friendship, and thanked me for my contributions.

The fact that they both cared enough to do that for me meant a lot. At the time, I didn't realize how much. That was the last I would ever speak with either of them. I was notified later that day that their plane had crashed into a dirt lot, just up the road from the editing studio where we had all first met. Rich, Jack, and Phil West were all tragically lost.

I was devastated, as were their families and everyone else that had been so blessed to work alongside them or to know each of them as dearly loved friends. Wanting to honor my friends and having been so close to being on the flight myself, I felt a heightened sense of purpose to do what they would have done for my In-N-Out family had the roles been reversed. I dedicated myself to providing anything my In-N-Out family needed—and to support close family members left behind.[11]

In another twist, in the days following Rich's death, it became clear that before the crash he'd had a strong sense he was going to pass away. More than one person has told me this, underscoring the truth of it. Here's how In-N-Out executive Mark Taylor put it.

What's strange is that Rich had been basically telling people that he was ready to go. He said that if he died tomorrow, it would be okay. He said he was good with God. It didn't make any sense to me at all why he kept saying that.

Before he went to the Fresno store opening and to see Guy and Lynsi, he met me at Store Number 64. I always felt like Rich respected me as a manager, and I know he loved my wife, Lynsi's sister Traci, to pieces (if you know my wife, you love her). I really felt like he was genuine in our relationship.

So, he met me at Number 64 in the dining room and said to me, "Mark, how is Guy doing?"

I looked at him and said, "He's never been better."

He was like, "Really? I need to know, how is he doing?"

I told him the truth. Guy was never better than he was right before the crash. The times I'd been up to the ranch in Northern California, Shingletown, he was as happy as he was the entire time I knew him. When Guy had lived in Southern California, he'd been angry about the way his father had left things. But once he was away, up there with Lynda and Lynsi, he was finally at peace. He was being a good man and he was just a pleasure to see.

So, I told Rich all that. I know Rich made a real effort to see his brother then.

At the time, it was hard for our family and the In-N-Out family to see past the devastation of losing Uncle Rich, Jack, and Phil. Yet the company had to be led. Our company had been experiencing tremendous growth. Under Rich's leadership we'd grown from eighteen stores to ninety-three. He'd been instrumental in setting us up for future success, adding an even greater focus on our associates and solidifying the In-N-Out brand.

As we grieved, the big question was, Who would lead our company now?

Chapter Eight

GUY AT THE WHEEL

He has delivered us from the power of darkness and conveyed us into the kingdom of the Son of His love, in whom we have redemption through His blood, the forgiveness of sins.

COLOSSIANS 1:13–14

THE LEADERSHIP ANSWER WASN'T IMMEDIATELY CLEAR. RICH HAD served as In-N-Out's president and driving force for more than seventeen years, since the passing of my grandfather in 1976. Esther, as secretary-treasurer, knew the business as well as anybody, but she was seventy-three when Rich died and didn't want the lead job, at least not alone. Nobody wanted to sell In-N-Out Burger, even though offers started coming in.

A workable arrangement soon emerged. My grandmother became president, although it was mostly an honorary title. My father became executive vice president and chairman. Essentially, it meant that my father would run the company. He was sober then, doing well, trying to put God first in his life. He pledged loyalty to our long-standing traditions of quality, freshness, and putting the customer first.

It must have been a shock for my father to be placed so immediately in such an important role that he'd never envisioned. Though he'd never expected or asked for it, his instincts, training, and values kicked in, and he grabbed the challenge and rose to the responsibility. He committed fully to supporting his mother and leading the company through this unbelievably difficult and challenging time. Priority one for Dad was to steady the ship.

He began regularly appearing on BTV episodes, walking everyone in the company through the grief, and encouraging all to take heart in God's comfort, purposes, and plans. Dad had an uncanny way of inspiring people, pulling our teams together through his presence and personality. Turned out he had a huge heart filled with empathy and a gift for communication. On one BTV broadcast he vowed, "No tragedy or disaster can stop the Snyder family and associates at In-N-Out Burger. You can count on that."[1] He made sure the flags at company headquarters flew at half-staff while the In-N-Out family took time to mourn. He was real and raw.

Guy put expansion briefly on hold to focus attention on supporting existing stores. He assured store managers that he trusted in their ability to carry out my grandparents' vision. He placed a particular emphasis on the importance of each individual who worked for the company, and he went out of his way to help everybody feel seen and valued. "Sometimes you might be working and thinking, 'I might not be noticed,'" he told associates in a BTV broadcast. "Believe me, you are noticed, and you're very important to us. You're our future. I want to thank you for that."[2]

Slowly, he began to weave his love for muscle cars into the In-N-Out story, using it to look beyond the tragedy and get everyone excited about the future. He and his cars were routinely featured on BTV as he shared updates and important company information.

State-of-the-Art Moves

Whereas Rich had his eyes on the future, Dad focused on mastering the basics: quality, friendliness, cleanliness, and quick service. Though Harry and Guy had disagreed on some things, they perfectly aligned on the recipe for In-N-Out's success: deliver quality food to the customer and be dedicated to our people.

Dad invested heavily in our quality assurance team. He went to great lengths to ensure that our warehouse and meat department accepted only the freshest and highest quality products for delivery to the stores. He put into place new state-of-the-art quality controls. He cared deeply about continuing to provide customers with the best-tasting burgers and fries in the business.

"We take pride in everything we do by serving a quality product with excellent service with a smile," Dad said.[3] There was that long-proven In-N-Out magic trio: product, service, smile.

The hamburger bag from 1990.

At one point Dad discovered that our grills couldn't keep up with the volume our stores generated. As a solution, he doubled up on the heating components so our grills cooked with consistent heat. That allowed more burgers to be cooked at the same time. Soon afterward a better brand of grill was found and presented to him. Even though he'd just spent money retrofitting old grills, he said, "It's a better grill and it will cook 50 percent more meat. Let's do it."[4]

The new grill worked well, but it was a little deeper front to back and had room for four rows of meat instead of three. That extra space was great, but that space came out of the bun-toasting area, and he had to find a way to toast buns faster. Those toasted buns are important. In-N-Out buns are the best, and the slight caramelization of the toasted bread lends to that signature In-N-Out taste. With the new grills, Dad needed to figure out a new grilling ratio of burgers to buns.

Dad enlisted Howard Frantz, director of research and development, to help solve the patty-to-bun ratio puzzle. One afternoon, Howard was studying the matter with executive Carl Van Fleet. As an aside, Carl described to Howard a recent trip he'd taken with his kids to a museum. The museum's pinboard display captured the children's imagination. When kids pressed a hand or any small object on top of the display, dozens of flat-head flexible pins formed a three-dimensional replication.

"I think we can use that idea!" Howard said. He developed a brilliant bun toaster based on similar principles. The ratio puzzle was solved and the invention patented. They referred to it as the bun clamshell. My dad loved the idea. He was all about innovation. Since then, we've developed a newer version of the bun clamshell that's easier to clean and includes a timer. Our bun toast continues to be one of the most important things about making a perfect burger.

Family Style

Dad stayed true to his pledge to ensure everyone at In-N-Out felt loved and valued. In early days, employees had been called "helpers," then Rich had coined the use of the term "associates." But my dad preferred to speak of everyone at In-N-Out as "family." He went to great lengths to make every person feel heard and appreciated.

What's So Great About an In-N-Out Bun?

You can't create a great-tasting hamburger without a great-tasting bun. And my grandfather believed in toasting. A properly toasted bun was so important to Harry that he built it right into the first of his four essentials of cooking, a method he handed down to all his helpers.

In early years Harry experimented with at least six bakeries before going with one that met his standards. All the bakeries we use bake our buns with old-fashioned sponge and dough, and they all use granulated sugar to attain Harry's vision of a properly toasted bun. He was proud that he didn't use any chemical additives to speed the process.

Why is sponge dough the superior choice? Sponge dough provides a good fermentation process and a unique flavor and aroma. The finished product tastes great. The natural granulated sugar included in the recipe allows for a perfect caramelized toast. And no preservatives are used.

But the advantages of sponge dough are hard-earned. Due to the natural yeasts used, there is a slim margin for error. Also, sponge dough has a much longer fermentation and production time, which vastly increases the need for equipment and space. Granulated sugar is also much more expensive than the liquid sugar used in other buns.

As always, however, for Harry the high product quality resulting from using sponge dough to bake these buns far outweighed the cost in effort and expense. This aligned with his business philosophy. "At In-N-Out, we will never sacrifice quality for price."

Rich Snyder spending time outdoors with the
original Club 48 members in Montana.

My father made it a priority to regularly gather everyone in the company together. When it came time for company picnics, he flew the Las Vegas and Northern California people to Orange County so we could all be together. He didn't always do this, but it was a bold move that showed his heart, and it endeared him to many. Each year he took divisional managers and department heads to Montana for team-building and planning events, which strengthened bonds and created memories together. It was a small group back then—the original Club 48, which we still have today. It had stopped when my dad died, and I brought it back around 2009.

Where Rich had worked to maintain his image as a professional, according to executive Wendell Ansnes, Guy considered himself more one of the gang. He did away with shirts and ties, and "he ran the store a little differently. But he saw things that others didn't—he was always looking at the speed of service and quality," Wendell said.[5]

Quality and taste were super important to Dad. My father worked on perfecting processes, just like Harry had done. During his tenure Dad improved the fry table, the warehouse department, and the meat department. More than anything, he wanted to make sure all the associates did things right. He was a boots-on-the-ground-style leader and regularly talked with associates, listening to their input. He built on what his father and brother had achieved, continuing to attain higher levels of quality and service for In-N-Out guests.

Every chance he got, Guy voiced his appreciation for the In-N-Out family and how each person contributed to the company's success. One of my favorite video recordings of my dad from that era captures his heart. In it he says, "You've made this company great. I'm proud to be part of it, and my mom is very proud too. No other company has the effort and the camaraderie and the love that we have here at In-N-Out Burger."[6]

Expansion Under Guy's Leadership

Dad believed like my grandfather did in paying cash for everything rather than borrowing for capital improvements. This policy slowed the growth to a pace somewhat behind what Rich had planned, but that suited Guy fine. He focused on building stores in high-traffic areas. After a time, he resumed expansion into the Bay Area and Northern California all the way up to Redding and into Arizona. "We feel that if we can keep our product and everything else about our company the way it's been going since 1948," he said, "we will be prepared to go on to the year 3000."[7]

I don't think my dad had ever envisioned coming into leadership of the family business to such an extent. He'd been content to leave all that behind. Even so, after Rich's death he led the company to new levels of success and prosperity while extending gratitude and respect to his In-N-Out family. "I wish my father could see what we've become today," he said. "I want to thank each and every one of you for making this company what it is today."[8]

In 1994, Guy oversaw the opening of the corporate office building in Irvine that Rich had purchased. In-N-Out occupied the top two of ten floors (today we fill eight floors). That same year we reached the milestone one hundredth store, opened in Gilroy, California, at 641 Leavesley Road. In a touching move, Dad dedicated the store to Rich. I was there. It was such a wonderful celebration that the mayor of Gilroy proclaimed it even better than the opening of the new Gilroy City Hall.

In 1996, Guy brought the BTV production in-house and asked the highly capable Bill Scherer to lead the department. "It was a true honor to be offered such a wonderful opportunity, and I quickly accepted," Bill recalled years later.[9] Guy brought his own unique focus to the show's content. Under Guy's leadership, Bill created a company-wide training segment, a history- and culture-based piece called "The In-N-Out Time Machine," and "The BTV Burger Bowl," which fused informative content with high-entertainment segments that became well-known. Today BTV has an internal crew of experienced industry professionals and also uses independent production teams. At times the scope of productions has been so amazing that BTV segments have required full sets packed with cast and crew. Now we are streaming BTV monthly to the store's mobile devices that connect to the TV.

What could be a better location for a burger stand than right smack beside a university campus? Dad grabbed that vision and on April 1, 1997, our 119th store opened at 922 Gayley Avenue in Westwood, adjacent to the UCLA campus. Designed by acclaimed architect Stephen Kanner, the building's unique pop-art look and angular layout stands as a tribute to 1950s jet-age architecture. It offered a cheerful new twist to In-N-Out stores, and my father loved its look.

In November 1998, we marked In-N-Out Burger's fiftieth anniversary. Both Dad and my grandmother spoke at the celebration, recalling with emotion how the company had grown from a tiny hamburger stand in Baldwin Park to 132 stores with more than five thousand associates. "We owe a lot to you," Esther said tearfully to the crowd of associates. "I want to thank you from the bottom of my heart. I'm sure Harry and Rich are smiling down from heaven."[10]

To mark the occasion, a commemorative T-shirt was designed by artist Mark Davidson. It featured a classic 1950s-era woody wagon in front of an In-N-Out drive-thru and the original store sign reading "In-N-Out Hamburgers: No Delay." (Later, artist Mike Rider designed a shirt for 2001 that also featured a woody wagon along with other cars at Store Number 119 in Westwood, with California, Nevada, and Arizona in the background.) An actual woody wagon was given away in a drawing at the anniversary.

The lucky winner was astounded. He thought he had entered a contest to receive a model of a car.

That day in 1998 was such a high point, but as happy as it was, the celebration was short-lived for our family. My grandmother's health slowly began to decline, and this was only the beginning of a season of rough waters for our family. Esther needed to pull back from her daily responsibilities. Even then, she remained a force and a beloved figure at In-N-Out. As associate Jon Peterson recalls, "At new store openings, Jeff Helmrich would drive Esther over. The associates would visit with her while she sat in the car. Sometimes there was a line of thirty people waiting to talk to her. She wanted to see everybody. She was constantly doing things for us and making things pleasant."[11] We would be blessed to enjoy her stabilizing presence for a little while longer.

Life in Shingletown

After my uncle had died and my father had started to lead In-N-Out, he moved my mom and me from Shingletown back down south to Los Angeles so he could be closer to work. I was in the middle of sixth grade, and the move was hard on me. I had loved living up in Shingletown, where I was just another kid. But down in Los Angeles, the other kids figured out who my family was, and I was treated differently and picked on. I'd always had good grades before, but in Los Angeles my grades began to suffer. It was one of the hardest years of my life. After a year my father decided to move us back to Shingletown. Family was first for him. He would commute back and forth to Los Angeles for work.

Mom and Dad both wanted me to attend a Christian school, but the only one—where I'd gone for fifth and part of sixth grade—was an hour away. Mom and Dad talked to some other parents in the area and ended up purchasing an eight-acre property closer to our ranch. My parents secured a husband-and-wife team of accredited teachers and set up a homeschool program for me and a few other children in the area.

We gathered in a renovated house on the property. Desks were set up in a U shape, with everybody in one class. Computers were brought in. A ropes course was set up for our PE classes. I played every sport offered—coed basketball, soccer, rugby, flag football, tennis, frisbee golf, and hockey. When the snow fell, we went cross-country skiing. We called it Shingletown Christian Academy, and over the years it was a highly positive experience for me. I think we started with seven kids. The most we ever had was eleven. I ended up graduating from the school in a class of three, all girls, and the kids in that class went on to do amazing things.

The summer before we moved back up to Shingletown, I worked. I was twelve, and my dad let me help out at Store Number 3 in La Verne. I was too young to go through the formal hiring process at In-N-Out, but Dad agreed I was ready to get in there like he'd done when he was a kid. So there I was in the back room, washing dishes and doing produce prep. I was so nervous!

On my first day I faced one of my fears. I know—it sounds crazy today, but I was afraid of tomatoes. Something about their seeds, slime, and juices just freaked me out. I had to put them in the slicer and face that fear. The next day they let me pour drinks. I felt timid at first. It might be hard to believe, but I was shy back then. My nerves loosened up a bit once I got going. When Dad asked me what part I liked best, I told him I especially liked seeing the customers smile. It was a genuine thrill.

Everything to Know About In-N-Out Burger Soft Drinks

In 1948, when Harry and Esther founded In-N-Out Burger, the drinks came in bottles, as the technology for fountain drinks was still in its infancy. Instead of being listed on our menu, the bottles were lined up in the window along the single lane so customers could see their options.

At the time we offered eight soft drink flavors: both Pepsi-Cola and Coca-Cola, Hires Root Beer, 7UP, cream soda, orange soda, strawberry soda, and Delaware Punch. These bottles were stored in a refrigerated chest-style icebox to keep them cold. Helpers would retrieve the desired flavor from the icebox, open the bottle with a bottle opener, and provide straws, as needed, for any drink served.

At the end of 1958, a radical price increase in bottled sodas triggered a switch to fountain drinks served in a cup. Fountain drinks utilize soda syrup injected into a stream of carbonated water—a technology not invented until 1950 by Walgreens drugstores. Originally, we purchased cans of soda syrup, which were then opened with a can opener to fill the two-and-a-half-gallon canisters.

When Harry switched to fountain drinks in 1958, he eliminated five of the original eight flavors and went with his three best-selling flavors: Pepsi, Hires Root Beer, and Nesbitt Orange.

Pepsi remained the cola of choice until 1992, when Rich made the decision to go to Coke products.

Hires Root Beer was an independent brand but sold its bottling rights to both Pepsi and Coke in 1980. After that, we went with the root beer provided by Pepsi, and then in 1992, Coca-Cola—Mug, Ramblin', and Barq's.

Nesbitt Orange was not carbonated—it was more of an orange drink than a soda. It was served until sometime in the 1970s, when it was replaced with carbonated orange soda. In the early 1980s we stopped serving orange soda altogether.

Lemonade was added in the mid-1950s. It was sold in small cartons at first and then from the same style lemonade machine we use today. The original color was yellow. Red food coloring was added to make pink lemonade in the early 1970s, as a friend of

Harry's said it would sell better—and it did. Felbro Pink Lemonade became the standard in the mid-1970s, and we still work with them today.

7UP returned to the menu in 1975 due to a successful marketing campaign in 1974 that triggered customer demand for a caffeine-free option.

Diet Pepsi (Rich's favorite) appeared on the menu circa 1982 and remained there until 1992 when we switched to Diet Coke.

Freshly brewed iced tea (Lipton) was added to the menu in 1988.

After years of customers asking for Dr. Pepper (on our annual surveys), it was finally added to our menu on November 20, 1996. It was also Guy's personal favorite.

Minute Maid Lite Lemonade was added in 2011—it was re-branded Minute Maid Zero Sugar in 2020.

During the season after my dad began his leadership, things had been getting rough for him. Not long after the fiftieth-anniversary celebration, his difficulties would come to a head. Despite how well he was doing on the surface, things weren't going well in his private life. He'd been sober when Rich died, but my mother believes the stress of leading the company and losing his baby brother pushed him back into alcohol and drug use.[12] He began to exhibit mood swings and behavior changes. He had surgery on his back and took a lot of medication afterward. The stress of commuting got to him. Once, when I was twelve and visiting my dad for Father's Day where he stayed in Los Angeles, he was still medicated heavily from his back surgery. He fell asleep in the living room with a cigarette in his hand. I remember I had to grab it and put it out so the couch wouldn't catch on fire. Sadly, during that era he had an affair with a woman he knew in Los Angeles. I caught him on the phone and shared the information with my mom. Things became so difficult that my parents separated in 1995 and formally divorced two years later.

My mom kept the ranch in Shingletown, where I lived with her, and Dad moved to Claremont, almost nine hours away. Shortly after the divorce, Dad married the woman he'd had an affair with, but I didn't go to the ceremony. I wasn't close to his new wife, and it just seemed better not to be there. Overall, Dad wasn't doing well by then, and the second marriage wasn't a match. They divorced in the spring of 1999. Today, she and I are friends and have made amends.

After my parents divorced I still longed to have a close relationship with my dad. Our personalities were similar, very honest and real. We shared a lot of the same interests. He loved muscle cars, John Wayne movies, and driving the tractor at the ranch. So did I. We saw each other whenever we could, although it was never easy.

In 1999 I turned seventeen. I'd been working in a dentist's office, but a new In-N-Out store was opening in Redding, California, about forty-five minutes from Shingletown. Some people said the store was too far north; it would never work. But my dad believed in its location. I told my dad I wanted to work at the new store. He was willing just to get me in, but I didn't want to be treated any differently. For two hours I stood in line so I could apply. They accepted my application, and I went in for a second interview. I smiled with pride when I got the job. I went through the full training process, too, just like everybody else.

Since it was a new store, all new hires went through training together. I didn't tell anyone who my dad was. When I started on the job, I felt nervous and shy at first, but with each passing day I grew more comfortable. Working alongside fellow associates who shared the goal of making every customer happy in a spotless, sparkling environment bonded us. Whether I was refilling a drink, leafing lettuce, or cleaning tables till they sparkled—no job seemed too small or unimportant. Every detail mattered. I soon grew to love interacting with customers. It gave me a chance to make someone smile. The store ended up doing super well. When it came to my dad's business intuition, once again he proved right.

A Battle Lost

Ever since my dad's motorcycle accident, he had struggled with pain. One way he managed the pain was with drugs. They started catching up with him. From the time my parents divorced when I was twelve to when I was seventeen, I would sometimes go a full year without seeing him.

In the late 1990s, he was diagnosed with an incurable condition called porphyria. It's a rare hereditary disease where certain chemicals in your body stop changing as they should. His pain grew worse. He struggled with stomach problems and tingling throughout his body. Photosensitive blisters broke out on his hands. Apparently, stress and drug use can trigger and exacerbate symptoms, and the disease can even affect a person's mental health, prompting anxiety, confusion, and hallucinations.[13]

As his health declined, he resolved to safeguard the family company for future generations. In a statement to company associates that would become truly prophetic, my dad said, "If I have anything to say about it, your grandkids will be able to enjoy Double-Doubles."[14]

One morning in early December 1999, I was on my way to school when Dad called. I remember talking to him briefly and rushing him off the phone, not wanting to be late for school. That was the last time I spoke with him.

My father died on December 4, 1999. The immediate cause of his death was congestive heart failure, but there's no doubt his pain and drug use contributed. The Los Angeles County Coroner's Office, after completing the autopsy, declared his cause of death as an accidental overdose of hydrocodone,[15] which had caused his heart to give out. He was forty-eight.

I was devastated. I felt completely lost without my father. I was seventeen when he died, not even yet graduated from high school.

Dad's funeral was private and small, family only. My mother made the arrangements. Dad was buried at Forest Lawn Memorial Park. On his gravestone is inscribed, in part, "He touched many hearts and was treasured by his family," along with the words to Colossians 1:13–14, printed at the start of this chapter.

His death was a tragedy on so many levels. But he'd been a greater business success than anyone had ever dreamed. We held a large celebration of life for him at Pomona Raceway. He left a tremendous professional legacy, including the growth of In-N-Out Burger from ninety-three stores to 140. He had planned and developed our company's move into the Arizona market. He'd made innovative changes to cooking systems. Perhaps most significant and close to his heart, he'd been successful in keeping In-N-Out Burger private and focused on quality and freshness, ensuring that the company he loved so much would continue to be run as a family business at the highest level. I treasure the Guy Snyder legacy on so many levels, but mostly I treasure him as my dad. I miss him more than I could ever try to articulate.

Chapter Nine

ESTHER'S TEAM

Charm is deceitful and beauty is passing, but a woman who fears the Lord, she shall be praised.

PROVERBS 31:30

GUY'S DEATH HAD TO BE HARROWING FOR ESTHER. NO MOTHER wants to outlive her own children. Today, as a mother of four, I can't imagine that kind of grief. She was seventy-nine and president when my dad died in 1999, and Gram's health was in decline. She'd broken a hip a few months earlier, then suffered an infection during the healing process. Her strength wasn't what it used to be. By all accounts, my grandmother drew on her unshakable faith to get through the losses of her husband and both sons. A private woman, she could have become reclusive or shut everyone else out, but she remained in touch with the In-N-Out family like she had always done. As she soldiered on, she helped keep the company together by her will and her nature, offering comfort and compassion to everyone.

Those around her honored my grandmother and loved her for the way she handled her grief and the transition. Greg Fairchild, who was with In-N-Out from 1972 to 2019, summed up how so many of us felt.

Esther was one of the sweetest ladies you could ever meet. I feel blessed to know her. I think she knew all her store managers and divisional

151

managers by name. She always said, "Hi, Greg, how are you? How are Kathy and the kids?" I always found it easy to talk with her. I'd stop in at the office on a Saturday and Esther would be there working, going through the mail.[1]

Gram's support for the company and the In-N-Out family carried a lot of weight. She was universally loved and respected. As Donna Turkmani (1983–2012, retired from Cookout office manager) recalls,

> She was not only our supervisor, but she was also our mother, mentor, friend, confidante, and role model. Even though she had an upstairs executive office, she chose to be in the heart of accounting with the rest of us.
>
> We shared stories about our family and friends. She let all of us know that she cared for us and took an interest in our lives. She led by example and taught the values of good work ethics, hard work, dedication, honesty, and integrity.
>
> She also taught us the importance of giving back to the community. She took us to charity events and political events and got us involved in In-N-Out's Foundation. She set an example by being on the board of many local charities. She was looked up to by us all.[2]

That kind of quiet example spoke loudly, and I can't say enough good about my grandmother. Throughout all her years with the company, during hard times as well as good, she worked tirelessly, always embracing associates as family. Her genuine loving-kindness established the groundwork for a spirit of togetherness at In-N-Out Burger. She deserves a great deal of credit for the success of this company.

Executives and Trustees

During the era when Dad was alive and Grandma was president, many of the day-to-day operations of the company were entrusted to In-N-Out's team of executives. After my father died, many wondered what would happen to In-N-Out, but Grandma didn't worry. The team of executives kept things running smoothly, and several years passed without any hiccups.* She had no desire to sell the company. I was the only direct blood relative still living. But I was only seventeen when my dad died. For the next several years, there was no way I could run the company.

Personally, I struggled greatly after my father died. I mourned deeply, and with him gone, it seemed like my world fell apart. The security and love I'd felt from my dad was no longer there. During the years when he wasn't sober, I'd been longing that he would get better and that the security and love would return, but now there was no hope of that. So I dove into a deeply codependent relationship with my high school sweetheart, searching for the love and security I wanted from my dad.

At age eighteen, just out of high school, I married the guy. We had dated for four years by then. But for a number of reasons, the marriage didn't succeed. You've got to imagine: I was seventeen when my dad died in December 1999. I turned eighteen the following May. I graduated from high school in June. And I moved from Shingletown to Southern California and got married in July. I knew that we shouldn't have gotten married. But because of the deep loss and missing my dad, my grief propelled me into holding on to my boyfriend more tightly. He felt like the only source of love in my life.

I talk about these experiences candidly today, never to glorify my mistakes but to point the way forward for people who might find themselves in similar spots. Too many people are searching in all the wrong places for the deep needs of their hearts to be met. I've learned that only God can meet those needs. He offers love, security, and a true identity for his beloved children. In 2004 I went and saw the movie *The Passion of the Christ*. It made a big impact on me, and I put my mistakes behind

---

* Key among the team were Mark Taylor (1984–2020, retired as chief operating officer) in operations, Roger Kotch (1984–2018, retired as chief financial officer), Ken Iriart (1989–2013, retired as executive vice president of human resources), Carl Van Fleet (1990–2017, retired as executive vice president of strategic planning), and Arnie Wensinger (general counsel).

me and fully recommitted myself to God. I started a consistent pattern of going to church and Bible study. But these good decisions didn't happen overnight. After the divorce, I felt like a failure. I was only twenty years old. For about a year and a half after the divorce, I drank and smoked weed, struggling in many ways. Soon I jumped into another relationship that was not born of a healthy place. Though we both walked with God together for much of our relationship, it didn't start there. I plan to write another book in the future where I tell the full story of my life in detail, from failed marriages to deep realizations about my true identity. For now, please know that I've chosen to be honest about my mistakes, and I tell them in hopes of preventing people from going down similar harmful paths.

For a while, ownership of the company was held in trust, although that would become both a help and a hindrance. Mark Taylor, general manager and a trustee, was consistently reliable. He'd been with the company for years before my father died, and he was my older sister Traci's husband, so I'd grown up knowing him as family. Mark and I weren't related by blood, but I knew he always had my best interests at heart. He's like a brother to me.

At the time, there was someone else in a position of authority who I didn't know super well. After a few years, I developed a gut feeling that this person was also working to pit me against Mark, my own brother-in-law. I would be told things like, "Hey Lynsi, you want a Mercedes? I can talk Mark into you getting a Mercedes. I'm on your side. I'll take you to the dealership and work it out. I can help you get what you want." But there were always strings attached—strings that encouraged me to go to him rather than my family.

Meanwhile, word got back to me that there was an effort to prevent Mark from talking to me. They'd say stuff to Mark like, "Hey, you don't need to go to Lynsi. I can get her to do what needs to be done." It felt like this person wanted to keep me busy and out of the way.

At the start I didn't see it, and didn't realize how bad it was. When I finally grasped what was going on, I went directly to general counsel Arnie

Wensinger and said, "Something doesn't seem right. I think you need to look behind the scenes."

Arnie initiated an external audit of this person's business area. Where there was smoke, there was fire, and we set off the alarm. The executive team called a meeting and asked this associate for a resignation. The person agreed, then walked out of the meeting, hired an attorney, filed lawsuits, and started a war against the company.

It was horrible, and somehow I was caught in the middle. To make matters more difficult, I was also pregnant with my twins at the time. The newspapers printed terrible things based on legal filings, and they were complete lies. One headline insisted I wanted my grandmother to die so I could be president. It was vicious, cruel stuff, and I'm so relieved it's all behind us today. I thought it was one of the worst times of my life and a betrayal to my family. But I harbor no ill feelings and forgive him. In the end I am stronger because of it.

Legally, I can't talk about the resolution of the controversy, but to this day I'm grateful to Mark Taylor, Roger Kotch, and Arnie Wensinger. They all weathered the storm with me and displayed great strength and integrity. It was terrible, but we had each other.

Growth During Difficult Times

Remarkably, In-N-Out kept growing through the difficult seasons. Our executive team, managers, and associates were still firmly committed to providing quality and freshness with every meal served. The customer still came first. Our customers and vendors were still loyal to us.

On January 26, 2000, just over a month after my father died, we added a store in San Jose, about an hour's drive from San Francisco. We opened stores in Ontario, Bakersfield, Chico, Livermore, San Pedro, and Mountain View. We secured our presence in Arizona and over the next few years opened stores in Lake Havasu, Scottsdale, Avondale, Chandler, Mesa, Phoenix, Peoria, Prescott, Paradise Valley, Tempe, Kingman, and Yuma.

Our Meat Department

History of Our Wooden Beams (1989)

After our meat department was rebuilt in 1989, wooden beams were installed and placed above the checking and receiving rooms as well as the deboning room. The wooden beams were inspired by the look of a European meat market that Rich had seen and admired. We've always been proud of the fact that we use only the freshest, highest quality foods, and Rich wanted all associates—no matter if you were a store associate or a support associate—to have the same sense of pride.

To help remind associates in the meat department of our commitment to quality, Rich had a beam engraved with the words "We Accept Only Quality" added to the checking and receiving room.

In the meat department we use the phrase "When in doubt, kick it out." Every associate in the meat department is empowered to turn away anything that does not meet our standards. Each week some of the front quarter chucks are rejected and sold to someone else.

In the deboning room, Rich had a wooden beam engraved with the phrase "Fresh Every Step of the Way." Our commitment to this standard applies not only to our meat but to all the products we serve. This beam has been covered with stainless steel. The deboning room gets cleaned every day, and the water, over time, would have damaged the wood without the steel covering.

Similar large, engraved wooden beams grace our warehouses in Lathrop, California, and Lancaster, Texas. We put the ones from Baldwin Park in our new warehouse in Chino, California.

We loved our Nevada customers and opened stores in Henderson, Laughlin, Reno, Carson Valley, and Sparks.

In 2005, Rich's bold dream of two hundred stores was realized with the grand opening of the second In-N-Out location in Temecula, California. Four of the first customers to try the drive-thru arrived on horseback. Everybody cheered.

By August 2006, near the conclusion of the era when Esther and our executive team comprised the leadership, In-N-Out had opened a total of 202 stores. The company was thriving. The foundational commitments were all in place. We had no plans to sell the company or franchise. In-N-Out was the same quality restaurant it had always been, and we were looking toward a bright future. During those years, I had busied myself learning the ropes of In-N-Out Burger. I worked in carpentry, the meat department, and most other departments. I was a merchandise manager at our company store. I helped design T-shirts and catalogs. I loved the work, the associates, the customers, and the company. In-N-Out was in a good place, and I was learning the things I would need to know for my future role.

Making Grams Smile

That same month when we reached Store Number 202 in Petaluma, California, my grandmother passed away at the age of eighty-six on August 4, 2006. We held a private funeral. Pastor Chuck Smith from Calvary Chapel led the service. A number of people spoke, as did I, remembering Esther as a woman of tremendous personal integrity, courage, and compassion. She'd been a hands-on mother, warmhearted to everyone she met, and a terrific friend. She'd led In-N-Out with a true servant's heart, dicing potatoes and hand-forming meat patties, keeping the books, and making every customer feel special, mentoring hundreds of associates through the years and treating each one as family. Everyone who knew her loved her.

Esther was actually a business giant, although if you saw her, you'd just think of her as your next-door neighbor. A few days after she passed, a string

Esther with her son, Guy Snyder.

of the nation's largest newspapers ran articles memorializing her, including the *New York Times*,[3] the *Los Angeles Times*,[4] and the *Wall Street Journal*.[5]

As her granddaughter, what I treasure and will remember most about Grams is her generosity and compassion. She inspired me and countless others, pouring into our lives. She worked with the local branches of Boys and Girls Clubs of America, local schools, medical organizations, libraries, and more. She had a huge heart of kindness and cared deeply about children and their education. She was the driving force behind In-N-Out's philanthropic efforts. To this day the In-N-Out Burger Foundation carries out her compassionate vision. In her honor, we established the Esther Snyder Award in 2006 to congratulate an In-N-Out associate who goes above and beyond to fulfill the third part of In-N-Out's mission statement, making our communities safer, better, and more compassionate places to live. I can think of no more fitting tribute to a woman who exemplified true selflessness.

Esther always had a tremendous passion to help the next generation succeed. Back when Guy and Rich were in high school, they were friends with a youth around the same age named Wilbur Stites. They all enjoyed working on cars together. He'd been living at McKinley Home for Boys in San Dimas, but he did something to get kicked out and had nowhere to go. My grandmother took him in and fostered him for several years. Wilbur lived in my grandparents' pool house. When he was a bit older, she helped get him a job in the In-N-Out maintenance department.

Wilbur worked there for a good number of years and was soon able to buy a home of his own in San Dimas. He married and had a baby daughter. Tragically, Wilbur was killed in a car accident in 1979. My family was devastated. He'd become like another son. Wilbur was buried near my grandfather in the same family plot at Forest Lawn Memorial Park. My uncle Rich paid off Wilbur's house, and Esther took on the grandmother

A nineteen-year-old Lynsi spending time with her grandmother, Esther Snyder. They shared a love for sweets.

role for Wilbur's daughter, Meredith. Esther ended up putting her through college, then hired her in the accounting department, where she worked for several years until her mother moved to Chicago and she followed.

One of my favorite memories of my grandmother is about something that happened repeatedly when I was a little girl. I loved playing at her house on Covina Boulevard, not far from the very first In-N-Out Burger, Store Number 1. I would use her porcelain animal keepsakes to create a little world of imaginary circuses and zoos. The figurines were extremely breakable, but she never objected.

She'd give me her cute little giggle and say, "Oh, you're going to be an entertainer one day."

I wasn't sure what that might look like, but if it meant making Grams smile, that was all I needed.

Chapter Ten

THE THIRD GENERATION

Let us not grow weary while doing good, for in
due season we shall reap if we do not lose heart.

GALATIANS 6:9

WHEN MY GRANDMOTHER DIED IN 2006, I WAS TWENTY-FOUR—THE same age as Uncle Rich when my grandfather died and Rich became president. Did I want to step up and be president? I was asked, but I said no. It wasn't a question of commitment; it was a question of timing.

I was certainly active in the company. By that time I'd apprenticed in almost every In-N-Out Burger department including accounting, BTV, merchandising, carpentry, warehouse, fleet maintenance—you name it. But I'd just been through the toughest year of my life, dealing with several life-altering factors. I was grieving my grandmother's death. I was pregnant with my twins. Our legal battle continued on. I worked right up until the twins were born, then within a month I was back at work. I didn't feel the timing was right to take on the biggest business challenge of my life.

With no direct Snyder heir available to lead the company, we started getting a lot of offers from investors who were interested in buying the company and taking it public, but we kept saying no. There was no reason to sell the company other than money, and plenty of things are more important to us than dollars. Selling the company wasn't my grandparents' dream. It wasn't my uncle's dream or my father's dream. And it surely wasn't mine. Sometimes when companies are taken public, they do well and grow. But other times, a public offering can ruin a brand, radically change it, or compromise it so much that the company loses the very cornerstone they started with.

We wanted to preserve our traditional customer experience. In-N-Out has been wildly successful, and I believe it is one of the most trusted brands in the burger business today. No food at our stores is ever frozen, microwaved, or warmed. The pillars of service are kept simple—quality, friendliness, cleanliness. We wanted to keep doing what we do best: serving great burgers. Our customers trust us to do that, and I didn't want to make any change that would lose our customers' trust.

The family and leadership team decided that Mark Taylor should lead the company as president, along with an excellent executive team of people I trust and respect. Mark is my brother-in-law, after all, and he believes in the core values of In-N-Out in his heart.

Mark did a terrific job, continuing to grow the company. When he began to lead in 2006, we had 202 stores. Four years later, when we were ready for him to pass the reins, we had 239 stores. Mark was an excellent leader, and as part of his vision he'd led the company to expand into Utah.

On January 1, 2010, when I was twenty-seven, it was time for me to begin. Mark became the chief operating officer, and I stepped into the role of president of In-N-Out. People ask me if I felt ready. That's hard to answer. My intention was to lead the company with the same values that had been passed to me. Quality and freshness would always be important, and I had no plans to radically change the company. Serving the customer would always be first in my mind.

But I think if you wait until you're perfectly ready to do something, you'll never do it. I wish I could say it was easy from the start, but it wasn't. It's a tall order to lead a company. I determined to love everyone, listen hard, depend on all I'd learned so far, ask for advice when needed, and ultimately let God guide and defend me.

A New Style of Leadership

One big change I brought to In-N-Out culture was my leadership style. My grandfather was brilliant, but he was a workaholic. While he had a lot of good qualities, he established a top-down style of leadership. He expected others to work at the pace he set: never miss a day of work, never make a mistake, be task-driven and results-oriented. He insisted you do what you were told. While he was friendly, he didn't hesitate to raise his voice or yell. I wasn't going to be that type of leader.

Rich had learned from his father. In-N-Out was his life and identity. He lived and breathed In-N-Out. And while he did a good job of leading the company, it came with a personal price. He spent so much time in the office, it was hard for him to find an identity outside of In-N-Out. Rich had always wanted to make his father proud, even when Harry was no longer around. Toward that aim, Rich grew the company with everything he had, even when it cost him personally.

My dad had seen the leadership styles of his father and brother, but he didn't want that. Before he stepped into leadership, he could have chosen to be more closely involved in running In-N-Out. But he chose family life, at least when he was at his best. He left the corporate world behind to live with me and my mom on a ranch in Northern California with a lot of trees, wide open spaces, and running streams. I was seven when we moved there. Looking back now, it was the best thing my dad could have done for me. Those years in Shingletown were some of the best years I ever had with him. We lived in a modest home, raised chickens and goats, and drove tractors. I played outside and collected rocks and looked for obsidian. My dad and I rode quads and played hide-and-seek in a forest that spread over more than one hundred acres.

But my father had made his mistakes too. When it came time for him to lead In-N-Out, he felt the pain of loss and the pressure to lead an empire, and he turned to substances to cope. For many years, that's just the way it was. I didn't want that either.

When I became president, I hoped I had learned from history and would not repeat our family's past mistakes. I wanted the company to grow, but only in healthy ways. I began my tenure as president by asking, How can we make our In-N-Out family better? How can we encourage our associates to continue to serve our customers with quality and excellence? How can we make our customers happier without ever compromising or changing our core values? From the start, I had an amazing team of executives and managers who helped enormously. We would never compromise quality in serving our customers. We would work hard to listen to our associates and make sure each person was heard and valued.

Today, after more than a dozen years of being president, I can step back and evaluate. I can see that where and how I invest time is of utmost importance. It's true that I work a lot of hours, and sometimes I work during vacations or late at night. But I take time to be present with family too—it's a huge priority. I've learned it's so important to take time to recharge. I've seen people I love who work too much and then regret the things they missed. I made some of those mistakes early on.

Time invested in the company is important too. Success, to me, is about prioritizing what is most important, then making sure that shows in my life. With my associates, I'm always honest and vulnerable. I'm pretty much an open book, and that seems to foster an environment of others being real and open. So we share a bond, a connection, and a trust.

Leading the company hasn't all been easy, that's for sure. Even after I became president, drama from personal relationships distracted me from my kids and work. Ultimately I've come through those seasons, and I'm in a much healthier place today. The obstacles have been overcome, and they've made my faith stronger. Let me see if I can explain this more fully.

The Hard Years

My father's death when I was seventeen rocked me to my core. It felt like my best friend, protector, and defender was gone. I experienced an aching void in my life, so I sought to fill that void by seeking love and security from others. When my high school boyfriend and I headed for the altar, I was only eighteen. I already knew the relationship was risky. A still, small inner voice said, "Don't do this, Lynsi," but I did it anyway. I ignored that voice. The wedding ceremony took place a couple of months after we graduated. Two years later, I paid the price with a divorce.

I've mentioned that I was only twenty at that time. I felt embarrassed and ashamed, and to make matters worse, the aching void was still there. In fact, I felt even more alone than ever. Plus I started to see myself as tarnished, like I'd become the family outcast. Truthfully, they didn't treat me that way. But for a time, I figured I just embraced being the outcast. I started smoking pot and drinking with my new boyfriend too much—things that I'd wanted to avoid after watching my dad's struggles.

Again, the relationship was rocky. I met a pastor and his wife who helped me realize I would soon follow in my father's footsteps and meet an early death if I didn't get right with God. I let go of the weed and alcohol, but letting go of the guy was more difficult. I was so afraid to be alone. I prayed, begging God to give me strength to break up with my boyfriend. Finally the guy and I had the hard conversation. But when I told him I wanted to get on track with God and did not want to continue my destructive ways, my boyfriend's response was to come full circle months later and turn his life over to God. I thought, *Okay, how convenient. Now we can get married.*

We took the fast track to the altar, but years later it became clear that wasn't the best choice. I know God changes people's lives, but he often changes them slowly, and the person needs to *want* to change. Unfortunately, that wasn't my second husband's story. I was struggling too. I was starved for love in the marriage and made a series of bad decisions, which ultimately led to us divorcing after six years of marriage. I don't regret the marriage, because I have two precious children from it, but getting divorced for a second time made me feel like an even bigger failure. I was alone again and even more damaged.

I soon found myself in another marriage, but it wasn't easy. I became pregnant, and after I gave birth I hoped things would change for the better, but they didn't. With my third marriage struggling, I experienced the lowest time in my life. I was being hurt in a way I'd never known before. I thought I deserved it. In that desperate time, I really started listening to God. I began to understand that God was not punishing me. As I listened, he showed me that he was there with me in my hurt all along—loving me, carrying me. He wanted to fill the aching void in my life. He was inviting me to fully say yes to him.

Meanwhile, my third husband and I couldn't fix our marriage. We finally divorced. After my third failed marriage I finally knew I needed to take some time and be alone. I'd been afraid of this for so long, but I discovered that time alone can be amazing. This was a special experience, just me being with God. This was the same Jesus who had walked on water, healed the sick, and made blind people see. That same Jesus was touching my heart, pouring into who I was called to be, filling the void I'd been furiously trying to fill for so long. Jesus loved and accepted me just as I was, and he wanted me to fulfill all the potential I had within me. He saw the real me, not the piece of trash I believed I was because of all the things I'd done.

When I finally realized the depth of God's love for me, that's when I was truly able to feel secure. It was a little like when you're a kid and your father shows you how to ride a bike for the first time. He's running alongside you, always there if you need him, never letting you get too far away. That's how I felt with God. He was showing me a new way to live. Truly free. Truly loved. Truly held in his arms.

It wasn't that all my grief about my own father magically disappeared. I certainly kept missing him. I miss him today. All the good times I had with my dad—laughing, watching cartoons, playing in the backyard, riding in something with an engine, feeling so safe in his care—those memories still make me sad that he's gone. But his love, as special as it was, can't begin to compare to God's love for me. What's also gone now is the sharp desperation I felt in the wake of my father's death. That's part of what's changed. God has given me a new peace.

It's funny, but once I started believing I didn't need a relationship with a man to feel whole, I felt free to start praying for a relationship. But if there was to be a new relationship, I wanted it to be different from all the others, not characterized by desperation. It would be a relationship of mutual love, respect, and caring.

When I met Sean Ellingson, things were completely different from the start. We both recognized that the other person was centered on God. We didn't need each other to be everything, because individually we had everything in Christ. Sean had served in the army, then headed through art school after he was out. And he was at a good place in his life—really ready for responsibility and love and children. He wasn't a fixer-upper. I didn't feel like I had to change him, as I'd felt with the others. He's a spiritual

With her husband and best friend, Sean Ellingson.

leader, and we were in agreement about so many different areas from the very beginning.

During our first talk on the phone, we waded into deep conversation. I mean, we didn't hold anything back. We talked about God and where we each were spiritually. We talked about what we both wanted in life. We talked about politics, and about him being in the military. He'd lost a younger brother to drugs. My father had struggled with addiction. At the end of the conversation, we each picked three things to pray about for the other person. Our relationship started in a really good place.

We were married in 2014 when I was thirty-one, and we've never looked back. Our love continues to grow and deepen, and our children are able to see that I'm grounded in the Lord and have my priorities straight. That's what matters for me now. Sean and I just celebrated our ninth anniversary, and we're more in love than ever.

Leading Today

Looking back over my young adult years, I see that my personal challenges and my growth through meeting and overcoming them has made me stronger. I've been humbled more than once, that's for sure. But I've seen that leading with humility can be a good thing. In my job today, I find that I spend a lot of time learning. I try to continually put myself in the shoes of others. And I see myself, even in the position of president, as a servant. It's my job to serve others and help anyone I can.

When people ask me what kind of leader I am today, I explain that I practice servant leadership. (I say "practice" because I don't always get it right.) Servant leadership means I treat others the way I want to be treated, with dignity and respect. I long to protect others the way I wish I had someone to protect me when I was choosing my way of destruction. Servant leadership means recognizing and engaging the whole person. I don't merely look at a person's work performance or provide a paycheck to them. I see each individual as a person. At In-N-Out Burger, we talk a lot

Mark Taylor started his In-N-Out career as an hourly associate, and worked his way up to chief operating officer of In-N-Out Burger.

about teamwork and how we care for one another. My goal is for each associate to succeed both in this company and in life. We are united, knowing we have each other's backs.

I'll be honest, shifting In-N-Out's leadership culture hasn't been easy. A top-down leadership style had become ingrained, almost second nature, for years. It's felt like I've been turning a large ship slowly, carefully. But I believe we've been successful. The leadership we now have on the executive team really embodies that servant leadership mentality.*

Many longtime associates have shared that the environment has radically changed for the better since I've been in leadership. That's encouraging.

---

* I'd like to give my executive team a little shout-out here: Arnie Wensinger, executive vice president, chief legal and business officer; Denny Warnick, executive vice president, chief operating officer; Mike Mravle, executive vice president, chief financial officer; Rob Howards, vice president of technology and business operations; Alex Frumusanu, vice president of quality and supply chain; Mike Cowan, assistant vice president of operations; George Charlesworth, assistant vice president of operations; Katie Sauls, vice president of human resources; and Mike Abbate, assistant vice president of real estate.

I know my family would be proud that we have found a way to reach our goals while encouraging others and maintaining high standards.

If you'll allow me a humblebrag, here is something my mentor Mark Taylor said about me and my leadership style, and it has meant the world to me. It's something I look back to for encouragement on my worst days, and I'm glad I have it written down.

"Lynsi's leadership is so different from mine—and it's the right leadership for the right time. She's made us kinder and more loving, which is her style. What she does as a leader amazes me. I really think she's going to be a household name. She just gets it on a different level. She's brilliant."

Well, I'll take that any day!

While the style of leadership at In-N-Out has changed, discipline and standards are still important, of course. We're committed to maintaining the highest standards, and the difference is that we try to do it in consistently healthy ways, showing grace and understanding.

Faith in Action

I came to my faith early in life, thanks to my mom and dad taking me to church. Today my faith is strong, having been tested by tragedy and loss. It's also been tested by my own choices and the consequences of those choices. I've accepted my God-given purpose inside and outside of In-N-Out Burger.

Today, I lean on God as I lead In-N-Out. I share my faith openly, and because of my faith I want to do something purposeful and helpful in the world. Prayer is a regular part of my interaction with my team. One great thing about a private family company is that I have freedom to speak openly about my Christian walk. It's a huge blessing, and I see a kind of practical faith showing up in everything we do at In-N-Out Burger. We treat others the way we want to be treated. It's as simple as that.

Here's one example of what practicing faith looks like. My heart breaks for people who hurt, and I want that heartbreak to motivate me and others to help change the world and save lives. In 2016, Sean and I started another official nonprofit organization for In-N-Out Burger. We call it the Slave 2 Nothing Foundation, and it exists to fight substance abuse and help stop human trafficking. Our mission is to help free people from being enslaved to any person or substance.

Back on our first date, Sean and I had talked about how destructive addiction can be and how people we had known and loved had been enslaved and tragically hurt or killed by substances. Because of our own losses, we wanted to join that fight along with anyone struggling against addiction and with those who have lost family members to the same.

Once we started to look into the issues more closely, we also saw that just as addictions enslave a person, so does human trafficking. At the start I didn't know much about human trafficking, particularly how much of it happens here at home. More than ten thousand people are trafficked each year in the United States alone. California and Texas have the highest number of human trafficking cases in the United States.[1] Children, teens, and adults, both men and women, are all sold. They're tricked or coerced into prostitution, commercial sex acts, or forced to do menial jobs. From then on, that's the only life they know. People are objectified and hurt and even killed. It's modern-day slavery, and none of us can ever be okay with people being treated that way. Today slavery is happening to all races all over the world. People are never supposed to be owned. It's horrifying and tragic.

So we aimed to spread awareness and help save lives. We wanted to be a voice for the voiceless and to help fight for people's good. Each year since then, Slave 2 Nothing has offered grants to carefully vetted, like-minded organizations located in the communities we serve. We help fund preventive measures, rescue efforts, and holistic rehabilitation centers that provide restoration and healing from the trauma experienced by victims.[2]

Sean and I have also started another nonprofit initiative, which we call the Army of Love. It's more overtly faith based, and we seek to bring together Christians who are called into more organic sorts of ministries. For our volunteers, we provide counseling, mentorship, and training in personal ministry. We hope to help them reach out and help heal brokenhearted people. We're just getting started, and we know the best is yet to come.[3]

Just as I've come out of hurt, I'm convinced that leadership gives me the responsibility to serve others in helping them come out of hurtful situations. I want everybody to fulfill their full potential, and I want In-N-Out Burger to be a company that offers hope.

Chapter Eleven

WHAT WOULD MY
FAMILY WANT?

Let us hold unswervingly to the hope we
profess, for he who promised is faithful.

HEBREWS 10:23 NIV

IN-N-OUT BURGER REACHED A MOMENTOUS MILESTONE ON October 22, 2023: our seventy-fifth anniversary. We're celebrating in style, and we're so thankful to our customers, vendors, associates, and leaders for their love and support over the years.

As we enter the fourth quarter of our first century in business, the thing that continually guides me is a straightforward question: What would my family want? In-N-Out has been a private, family-run company from the beginning. We continue to receive regular offers to take In-N-Out Burger public or franchise it, and while we see those offers as compliments and we appreciate them, for years our stance has been a polite but firm no.

So we'll stay true to our roots. We're not going to build new stores simply to make money. We'll grow only as we're able to ensure fresh supplies for each store. To maintain our high standards, we're determined that every single In-N-Out Burger store will be within driving distance of one of our warehouses. And it's not just about fresh ingredients. It's about people. We also want to ensure that the right leadership and support personnel are integrated into our infrastructure as we grow.

Cutting the ribbon at the new In-N-Out warehouse in the city of Chino.

Personally, I continue to be deeply involved with every aspect of the In-N-Out family business, overseeing daily operations, marketing, merchandising, event planning, associate engagement, company expansion, culture, leadership training, designing stores, and more. I've been super intentional about gathering our associates, building trust and a team atmosphere, and focusing on the right things to engage our people and get them committed to caring for our customers at the highest level possible. For me it's all about maintaining the legacy my family created and carrying us into the future with every important part still intact. I love this job, and I love In-N-Out.

The Legacy Continues

The most recent years for In-N-Out Burger have been marked by growth and success. Highlights include our expansion into Texas in 2011 with two

In-N-Out stores opening on the same day in Allen and Frisco. A brand-new warehouse and patty-making facility opened in Dallas, ensuring that these new restaurants, and others to follow, can guarantee the same quality and freshness enjoyed by stores close to our original Baldwin Park facilities. Even though the Texas market began under my leadership, it was really Mark who had established the groundwork for this specific growth. He receives the real praise here. While this was happening, I was planning for other markets that we'd open in the future.

On January 7, 2015, we opened our three hundredth restaurant—the second store in Anaheim, California. The opening date was special because it would have been my grandmother's ninety-fifth birthday. It's gratifying to see her legacy continue.

For years our good friends in the Pacific Northwest have been asking us to head northward. We took a solid first step in that direction on September 9, 2015, when we opened our first In-N-Out Burger store in Medford, Oregon, about a half hour's drive past the California state line on Interstate 5. The date marked what would have been my grandfather's 102nd birthday.

Inching northward, we opened a store in Grants Pass, Oregon, in 2017 and in Keizer, Oregon, in 2019, about a forty-five minute drive south of Portland. In 2022, we opened in Roseburg, in scenic southwestern Oregon. With us being so close to Washington State now, it's feasible that we will get there sometime soon, too, although we're not there yet.

In 2018, I took a bold step and adjusted our menu, bringing back hot cocoa. It wasn't a complete break of protocol because we first offered cocoa in the 1950s, although we stopped the trend in the late 1970s. Our newly introduced version is made with quality cocoa from the Ghirardelli Chocolate Company, and it's served with marshmallows. Yum.

Together with my team, I began studying our menu on the most intricate level to see if we could improve quality even more, making items better and healthier. We discovered a number of practices we were using were outdated. For instance, we worked with all our bakers to remove calcium propionate (a mold inhibitor) in our buns and replaced it with natural

Insider Tip: kids under twelve enjoy free hot cocoa on rainy days.

enzymes. With our chilis and pickles, we removed artificial Yellow 5 and replaced the additive with natural turmeric. In our strawberry shake syrup we removed artificial Red 40 and replaced it with natural fruit juice. In our vanilla shake we removed ethyl vanillin and replaced it with natural vanilla. In all our shakes and lemonade we cut out high fructose corn syrup and replaced it with natural sugar.

By now you know that In-N-Out Burger has always had strong ties to California's car culture. In 2018, *Hot Rod* magazine and In-N-Out celebrated our joint seventieth anniversary together at the Auto Club Raceway in Pomona. The celebration featured In-N-Out Cookout Trucks, a car show, and drag racing. The powerful connection with car enthusiasts continues to be a strong part of the In-N-Out heritage. We also hosted a party at Shrine Auditorium in LA featuring an amazing performance by the legendary rock band KISS. Our In-N-Out band opened for them (more on that band later).

On November 20, 2020, we opened our first two In-N-Out Burger stores in the great state of Colorado—in Aurora and Colorado Springs—both on the same day. We've since added stores in Lone Tree, Lakewood, Thornton, Castle Rock, and a second store in Colorado Springs.

In 2022, we unveiled a new educational assistance program called LEARN, offering it to all our associates. Under LEARN we help with tuition, fees, and books, reimbursing part of an associate's expenses in pursuit of a degree, professional certificate, trade or vocational program, or educational classes. I love that we can support those who want to grow while they continue working at In-N-Out, gaining new skills and increasing existing ones.

Always moving ahead, we opened another Utah store in August 2022, this one in Logan. (We'd opened our first in Utah in 2009.) Part of what made this opening significant was that a large, abandoned flagpole stood in the shopping center where the Logan store is located. Apparently another business had undertaken the efforts to correctly fly an oversized American flag but then abandoned the feat. It's no easy task. A Logan resident contacted us, asking if we'd be willing to fly and maintain an American flag on that empty flagpole. We were happy to help. Both my grandparents had served in World War II and they loved this country, as we do. So today flying over our Logan store you'll see a very large American flag—30 feet wide and 60 feet long. That's 1,800 square feet of flag—the size of a house!

In 2020, we launched a new event called Cruisin' 2 Freedom. Finding new ways to raise awareness and connect people together is a personal passion—and as you know, at In-N-Out, we're all car people. For Human Trafficking Prevention Month in January, we created the Cruisin' 2 Freedom Car Show and Cruise featuring vintage cars and classic sports cars. It was an incredible event that started at the Irwindale Raceway in 2020 with an

Driving her Chevelle in the Slave 2 Nothing
Foundation's "Cruisin' to Freedom" benefit.

auction and raffle, then we went for a cruise through the area around several of In-N-Out's original stores. In 2022, we held the event again, although this time at the Orange County Fairgrounds and participants went on a cruise through Orange County. These cars received a lot of positive attention. Picture cool old Chevy rat rods, Ford roadsters, classic convertible Mustangs, Porsches, Cadillacs, and souped-up pickups. Last year, I drove my red 1970 Chevelle SS in the cruise. The best part is that 100 percent of proceeds benefit organizations that create, educate about, and assist with solutions to eliminate human trafficking.

In 2023, we brought our connection to drag racing full circle, acquiring the naming rights to the Pomona Raceway. We want to keep the connection strong between In-N-Out Burger, drag racing, and the Snyder family. I know my dad would be proud.

Where's our next stop? Not long ago our executive team went with Sean and me to Franklin, Tennessee. We were special guests at a press conference with dozens of media. It was an exciting moment with Governor Bill Lee announcing that we will soon build our first corporate hub outside California in Franklin, Tennessee—the farthest east in our company's history. We'll soon begin construction on a $125 million facility that will employ about 270 people. From there, we'll be able to build stores further east than ever before. That news made a lot of people happy.

A Culture of Yes

One thing I'm particularly proud of is that I believe we've mastered what we call "a culture of yes." I didn't start it, but I worked hard to refine it and implement it throughout our company. The practice stems from our training and support teams, and essentially it means that we've pushed our focus on customer care a step further.

A lot is packed into that phrase. It's about giving the customer exactly what they want. Ask for a paper hat? No problem. It's yours for free. Want extra pickle, chili peppers, or well-done fries? All yours. With a culture of yes, we strive to say, "Yes, we can do that for you, no problem" as often as possible. Yes, you can even ask for a meatless burger option, although it's not on the menu. Just ask for a veggie burger, and we'll pile hand-leafed lettuce, tomatoes, and onions between two toasted buns. Yes, we can make it vegan, drop the spread, and substitute ketchup and mustard. Yes, you can get a Neapolitan shake by asking for chocolate, vanilla, and strawberry ice cream in one cup. Yes, we even have saltless patties for your pup if you and your dog come through the drive-thru.

Hand-Leafed Lettuce

If you ask for a veggie burger at In-N-Out, fresh lettuce will take center stage. When Harry Snyder started In-N-Out Burger, lettuce was not available in the many varieties that it is today. He opted to use iceberg lettuce, a variety still available.

Harry's 1954 training manual or "bible" never mentions putting ice on the lettuce before prepping. He was still selling bottled sodas at the time and didn't have ice. Once he switched to fountain sodas in 1958 and ice machines were added to all the stores, adding ice to the lettuce bath become our common practice. Harry felt it helped to keep the lettuce crisp.

The lettuce corer did not make an appearance until the early 1990s. Before that associates would remove the core by banging the core side of the lettuce head against the sink wall to loosen it and then pulling the core out of the head manually. We still hand-leaf our lettuce in clear view of the customer, essentially in the same way Harry did way back in 1948.

This culture of yes extends even further. On any given visit to an In-N-Out store, you'll meet associates trained to welcome customers with a warm smile and eye contact, open doors for you, grab high chairs for families with little kids, be patient and attentive when taking orders, never rush customers, hand out stickers to kids, and offer to refill drinks without being asked, all aimed to give you a positive experience. A yes experience.

If ever we need to say no, it might be for food safety reasons, or it might be something that would throw off our operation. Can saying yes slow the operation down from time to time? Well, *yes*. But saying yes whenever possible is part of who we are, and I believe our customers appreciate our willingness to go the extra mile. Like Uncle Rich always said, the customers are the ones who sign our paychecks. Our customer is our most important asset.

One specific way a culture of yes has impacted us relates to our In-N-Out Burger Cookout Trucks. For years at outside events we served burgers but not fries, and customers always asked about fries. We wanted our fries to be piping hot and fresh, made right on site. We could do that easily with burgers on a portable grill, but we couldn't figure out how to pull off fries. It was tricky to find a way to have fryers on trucks, because that oil needs to heat to 350 degrees to cook the fries and it doesn't cool down fast. We puzzled over this question for years. Finally, our terrific research and development team found the solution. It's all about a special lid that they designed, so we can now have fryers and hot cooking oil right on our trucks. So *yes*, we now serve fries!

Why the Best Potatoes Are the Best Potatoes

From the very foundations of In-N-Out, Harry Snyder wanted a fresh French fry to pair with his fresh, high-quality, made-to-order hamburgers.

Harry always selected the highest quality potatoes available and paid premium prices for the best. But the science of potato growing was not very advanced at the time, so he would use varieties such as russets or White Rose potatoes if they were the best available. Eventually his preferred choice became the Kennebec potato, as it was specifically grown for frying.

Years passed, and the original Kennebec potatoes were widely replaced in the industry by other varieties. We now use chip-stock potatoes, so named because they're specifically grown for frying potato chips. We buy the larger chip-stock potatoes, while potato chip companies purchase the smaller ones. Regardless, the potatoes we buy are always of the highest quality available.

Harry insisted that his peeled potatoes be diced by hand. Over the years, equipment has evolved to be more ergonomic and easier to clean, but we still dice our potatoes in clear view of the customer, exactly as Harry intended.

Although our potatoes were initially hand-peeled, the process was very labor-intensive. As fry sales increased, Harry began purchasing secondhand potato abrasion drum peelers from decommissioned navy ships. Harry learned more about proper potato storage, then added dedicated peeling and storage areas to the back room, rather than using outdoor storage like the shed at original Store Number 1.

Other restaurants are known to have as many as sixteen ingredients in their French fries. But not us. Our fries are made of the most basic, best-quality ingredients that French fries should have. Ours have only three ingredients—potatoes, salt, and sunflower oil. Fresh French fries are not typical in our industry, perhaps because it takes more care and effort to prepare them properly. But we continue to serve only freshly made French fries made from the highest quality, freshest potatoes possible, because we always want the best for our customers.

One of those fryers is in a truck that honors my grandmother. She always loved children. We created the Esther Snyder Cookout Truck, reserved for many children's and youth events in Southern California, although an event that features her cookout truck doesn't need to be focused solely on children. Anyone can rent the truck. It's equipped with two grills, generators, and a fryer. We're able to treat our guests to classic mini hamburgers, mini cheeseburgers, mini Double-Doubles, and yes, mini fries. The minis are cute, and they honor my grandmother because they're directed toward kids, even though any age can enjoy them. Every mini burger is cooked fresh to order and served in a box with a napkin. We also offer fountain drinks. A portion of the money raised by the Esther Snyder Cookout Truck goes to the In-N-Out Burger Foundation.

Mark Courtney, director of maintenance services, designed the kitchen area of the Esther Snyder Cookout Truck, and I worked with our marketing team to design the exterior. Some of our associates' kids are pictured on the side, and my grandmother's picture is featured on the back. In memory of her legacy, a portion of the proceeds support the In-N-Out Burger Foundation's efforts in providing help to children in our communities.

In-N-Out Keeps on Rocking

I love rock 'n' roll, and I find that music is a great way to connect people. Sean taught me to play bass while I was pregnant with our son in 2014. He's played guitar for a couple of decades, and he's really good. At first we just played together, then we added some fellow musicians from In-N-Out. We call ourselves .48 Special, an homage to the year In-N-Out began. Somewhere along the line we became the official In-N-Out band. We perform often at company gatherings, events, fundraisers, and picnics.

The band has changed its faces over time, but we have a core group of musicians, then rotate in a few singers and other musicians. I play bass and sing, and we come out on stage and dance with fire. Sometimes we have aerial routines. Sean plays lead guitar and rhythm guitar. Dave, our

The In-N-Out company band, .48 Special, having some fun with milkshakes during a photo shoot. I love working with them and playing music together.

drummer, is now one of my best friends, and most of our families in the band are pretty close. The band has become a family within a family. We're a cover band, and we play all the fun rock 'n' roll tunes people love to hear. We may have some originals in years to come.

Each year we produce a big concert called Rock 2 Freedom to raise funds for our Slave 2 Nothing Foundation. It happens in October, National Substance Abuse Prevention Month. For the last couple of years, we've held the concert at the House of Blues in Anaheim. People can sponsor a table or buy general admission tickets for a night of food and music. Every dollar raised goes to restore hope to individuals and their families impacted by addiction. It's exciting to have performances from rockers such as Jakob Nowell, Matt Bartosch, and HU3M3N. Our band, .48 Special, has played there a few times. Beyond the fun, we all believe so strongly in the mission. This important cause is close to our hearts. I love that we can have fun and do some good in this world at the same time.

I'm often asked if I get nervous before a performance, and the answer is

Lynsi sings and plays bass in the In-N-Out Burger company band.

Lynsi performing at a company picnic. It's a special time for
her to connect with associates and have fun together.

yes—but it's not so much about stage fright. What matters to me is doing my very best, whether I'm singing, playing bass, doing an aerial performance, or dancing with fire (or eating it!).

It's a mindset that transfers, because I want the best for you too. I want the company I lead to provide you with the very best experience each and every time you come into an In-N-Out Burger.

Today, in 2023, I'm proud to say that In-N-Out Burger has 391 stores in 7 states and 279 cities. As we inch toward our 400th store, staying privately owned is ingrained in our culture, because that's where my family's heart was and that's where my heart is too. We've been a family company from day one.

Starting with our first store in 1948, my family has tried to make every customer feel special. We want to serve you the highest quality of food. I can tell you that being seventy-five as a restaurant feels great! The goal has been and always will be for every In-N-Out customer to enjoy quality in every bite. We will continue to grow, and best of all we'll keep serving customers, taking care of each other, and helping those in our communities who are in need.

Back to that question, What would my family want? The answer is easy: continue our service the In-N-Out way without compromise for another seventy-five years—and beyond! God bless you!

OUR COMPANY PHILOSOPHY

In-N-Out Burger Mission Statement

In-N-Out Burger exists for the purpose of

- Providing the freshest, highest quality foods and services for a profit, and a spotless, sparkling environment whereby the customer is our most important asset.
- Providing a team-oriented atmosphere whereby goal-setting and communications exist, and to provide excellent training and development for all our associates.
- Assisting all communities in our marketplace to become stronger, safer, and better places to live.

In-N-Out Burger Cornerstones

Business Philosophy. At In-N-Out Burger, we maintain a high level of commitment to fulfill our mission statement in everything we do. In-N-Out Burger is an operationally driven company, striving to maintain a consistent image without franchising.

Product. At In-N-Out Burger our name, registered logo design, company colors of red, yellow, and white, and the number of items on our menu will not change. We will always serve only fresh—never frozen—high-quality products. Our spread recipe will be kept confidential, and the hamburger buns will never contain any preservatives.

Quality. In-N-Out Burger will never sacrifice quality for price and will continually inspect product to ensure that it meets our standard for quality. Our hamburgers and French fries will always be cooked to order and served using only quality ingredients.

Associates. In-N-Out Burger is committed to hiring friendly associates who possess the skills necessary to communicate effectively with our customers in fulfillment of our mission statement. In-N-Out Burger takes pride in offering all associates competitive salaries and wages, bonuses for managers, and consideration for promotion from within the organization for qualified associates.

Only the Safest Vendors

In-N-Out Burger is committed to purchasing goods and services only from vendors that strive to treat all employees fairly and maintain excellent labor practices. We uphold this commitment through the following policies:

- We require every In-N-Out supplier to affirm as part of our supplier agreement that it is not engaged in any type of human trafficking, human rights violations, or other illegal or unfair labor practices. As part of our supplier agreement, the supplier must also verify that it is not purchasing or using any ingredients in its products that originate from a nation or source engaged in forced labor, human trafficking, or other human rights violations.

- In all supplier contracts In-N-Out reserves the right to verify the supplier's compliance with this human rights policy, in addition to our safety and quality standards, through both announced and unannounced audits by In-N-Out or third parties working on In-N-Out's behalf. If any supplier is found to be in violation of these standards, In-N-Out intends to terminate that supplier's contract. Our standards are clearly communicated to each supplier prior to executing any new contracts.

- In-N-Out fully supports the California Transparency in Supply Chains Act and through these steps works to ensure that its suppliers comply with both its spirit and legal requirements. In-N-Out will immediately investigate and address any information brought to its attention regarding any actions by a supplier that may be in violation of this Act.

- Among the core values of In-N-Out are integrity, honesty, and respect. Through the hiring, training, and management of In-N-Out associates, we strive to enforce these values every day, ensuring that every person in our company is treated in accordance with federal, state, and local laws.

- In-N-Out associates who directly engage in supply chain management will be required to sign a document indicating that they fully understand and will follow these policies.

- In-N-Out trains associates to be responsible for its supply chain management principles underlying its standards, and provides education on how to identify and respond to supply chain issues, including potential issues such as human trafficking and other human rights violations.[1]

Our Commitment to Quality

From the first bite of your burger to your last French fry, quality is the most important ingredient at In-N-Out Burger. We don't freeze, prepackage, or microwave our food.

We make things the old-fashioned way.

Our commitment to quality starts with our hamburgers. And our burgers begin with our patties. Each patty is made using only fresh, individually inspected, whole chucks from premium cattle selected especially for In-N-Out Burger. Our team of associates removes the bones, grinds the meat, and then makes each patty.

We have always made our hamburger patties ourselves using only fresh, 100 percent USDA ground chuck—free of additives, fillers, and preservatives. We deliver them to our stores direct from our own patty-making facilities in Baldwin Park, California; Lathrop, California; and Dallas, Texas. We control the whole process so we can be certain of the quality and freshness of every patty we make.

Our commitment to quality doesn't stop there. All of our ingredients are delivered fresh to our stores. In fact, we don't even own a microwave or freezer. Our iceberg lettuce is hand-leafed. Our American cheese is the real thing. And we use the best available onions and the plumpest, juiciest tomatoes we can find. Our buns are baked using old-fashioned, slow-rising sponge dough. And we make every burger one at a time, cooked fresh to order.

Of course a great burger deserves great fries. At In-N-Out, French fries come from the finest, freshest potatoes. They're shipped right from the farm, individually cut in our stores, and then cooked in 100 percent sunflower oil.

Our shakes are just as genuine—made with real ice cream. At In-N-Out, that's the only way we'll ever make them. Because when you like to keep things simple, doing things the old-fashioned way is the freshest idea of all.

Insider Info #2

BIBLE VERSES ON
IN-N-OUT PACKAGING

(We print only the chapter and verse references on our packaging. Here's the full text of each verse.)

Milkshake Cups
Proverbs 3:5
Trust in the LORD with all your heart, and lean not on your own understanding.

Beverage Cups
John 3:16
For God so loved the world that He gave His only begotten Son, that whoever believes in Him should not perish but have everlasting life.

Holiday Beverage Cups
Isaiah 9:6
For unto us a Child is born,
Unto us a Son is given;
And the government will be upon His shoulder.

And His name will be called
Wonderful, Counselor, Mighty God,
Everlasting Father, Prince of Peace.

Coffee Cups
Luke 6:35
But love your enemies, do good, and lend, hoping for nothing in return; and your reward will be great, and you will be sons of the Most High. For He is kind to the unthankful and evil.

Hamburger Bag
Revelation 3:20
Behold, I stand at the door and knock. If anyone hears My voice and opens the door, I will come in to him and dine with him, and he with Me.

Double-Double Bag
Nahum 1:7
The LORD is good,
A stronghold in the day of trouble;
And He knows those who trust in Him.

Hot Cocoa Cups
John 13:34
A new commandment I give to you, that you love one another; as I have loved you, that you also love one another.

Fry Boat
Proverbs 24:16
For a righteous man may fall seven times
And rise again,
But the wicked shall fall by calamity.

Insider Info #3

FRIENDLY COMPETITION

At In-N-Out, we like to say our toughest competition is the closest In-N-Out store. That said, we love friendly competition among ourselves. Our stores compete against other In-N-Out stores in softball, soccer, volleyball, basketball, golf, Burger Bowl (In-N-Out trivia)—you name it. At the store and department levels, we incentivize our associates and stores to compete in the following categories:

- Burger volume increases
- Fry sales
- Excellence in food safety
- Warehouse choice (excellence in ordering accuracy)
- Lowest associate turnover
- All-star choice (excellence in supporting new store openings)
- Friendliest support associate
- Best service to the stores
- Operations choice (best support of the stores and store associates)
- Best trainer awards (highest performing managers in training and development of their teams)
- Plus, there's the Harry Snyder Award and the Esther Snyder Award.

The Harry Snyder Award

The Harry Snyder Award is awarded to an associate who exemplifies an outstanding contribution to the company by consistently demonstrating honesty, dedication, and pride in what we stand for. This person is someone who can be counted on to uphold the values of the company. This is one of the highest honors that an associate can achieve by working at In-N-Out Burger.

fun FACT

Each winner's name adorns one of our beautiful delivery trucks. When you see one of our delivery trucks out on the road, check under the driver and passenger doors of the cab to see if you can spot the name of the Harry Snyder Award winner.

1987: Mike Lomma

1988: Greg Patton

1989: Bob Lang Sr.

1990: Chuck Papez

1991: Phil West

1992: Ray Maldonado

1993: Bob Williams

1994: Esther Snyder

1995: Bob Lang Jr.

1996: Jack Ruley

1997: Kelly King

1998: Rich Snyder

1999: Guy Snyder

2000: Joe Gee

2001: Keith Brazeau

2002: Jaime Marquez

2003: Louis Marchesano

2004: Jeff Helmrich

2005: Ed Pendleton

2006: Wendell Ansnes

2007: Ken Kenwood

2008: Mark Taylor

2009: Dean Atkins

2010: Ken Iriart

2011: Ben Ruley

2012: Blande Pittman

2013: Paul Koshmider

2014: Marisa Garcia

2015: Ray Gonzalez

2016: George Charlesworth

2017: Roger Kotch

2018: Alex Frumusanu

2019: Denny Warnick

2020: Larry Littau

2021: Mike Cowan

The Esther Snyder Award

The Esther Snyder Award is another of the highest honors an associate can receive, and it's intended to recognize a current In-N-Out Burger associate who exemplifies the character of Esther Snyder. In addition to being a cofounder of our company, Esther was a servant leader, compassionate role model, and set the standard for giving at In-N-Out Burger. Her generosity and service to the community came with no desire or expectation of anything in return. While these attributes should be present while at work, the focus of the award is to celebrate those who go beyond work as they bring these characteristics into serving and impacting their communities.

2006: Adrian Alonzo

2007: Stephanie Westmyer

2008: Roger Kotch

2009: Tom Moon

2010: Greg Gillespie

2011: David Inocente

2012: Frank Nila

2013: Larissa Anderson

2014: Ellie Deckert

2015: Abbie Rust

2016: Kaitlyn Duncan

2017: Asia Alpher

2018: Leah Richter

2019: Kelli Kempt

2020: Lynsi Snyder

2021: Robin Doyel

IN-N-OUT BURGER AND
IRWINDALE RACEWAY

In-N-Out Burger and cars have always gone together like burgers and fries. Part of the association is quite natural. After all, as California's first drive-thru restaurant and pioneer of the first two-way speaker, In-N-Out helped set the stage for the car culture of the 1950s and 1960s in the heyday of the American automobile.

Many formative years of both Guy and Rich Snyder were spent at the Irwindale Raceway, a local but nationally known dragstrip in the 1960s and 1970s.

Drag racing started becoming popular after World War II, initially on backroads, dry lake beds, and abandoned airstrips. The National Hot Rod Association was formed in 1951 to legitimize the sport of drag racing. The stated purpose was "to create order from chaos" by instituting safety rules and performance standards. The sport grew and by the 1960s had a nationwide following.

Harry saw this as a business opportunity. In 1965, he purchased half-ownership of Irwindale Raceway, just a few miles from Baldwin Park. He put in two snack bars on opposite ends of the dragstrip. These snack bars frequently did as well as the main gate receipts.

Harry wanted to keep the two businesses separate so as not to tie the In-N-Out brand name he had been building for years with his new business venture. Initially he even had different helpers to staff the venues. That plan lasted for exactly one big event; quality and customer service suffered so badly with the new crew that Harry borrowed In-N-Out associates thereafter. Harry used to pay these incognito associates an extra dollar per hour to "work the drags," which ran every Saturday night, plus the weekends when bigger national events were in town. That extra dollar was a huge incentive at the time.

Guy and Rich were in their early teens when Harry put them to work doing odd jobs around the track. The teens ran elapsed times out to the racers, helped clean the snack bars, and picked up trash around the lot. Steve Gibbs, who later became vice president of competition for the National Hot Rod Association, was the track manager at the time. Years later he recalled this about the two boys: "They weren't spoiled little kids running around like you'd expect, being the owner's sons. They were good kids. I never had to get too hard on them. They did their work. That's the way I remember them. The Snyders had a strong work ethic. I think they wanted that for their boys too."

Around 1972, Harry sold his interest in the raceway, but in the interim, both Guy and Rich had fallen in love with the unique culture created at Irwindale Raceway, where great cars were paired with great burgers. Both brothers started racing cars when they were older as well as collecting and fixing cars of all varieties. Later, of course, Guy chose to follow his passion for racing while Rich followed his passion for the burger business; but both learned how to run a business and have a whole lot of fun at the same time.

HOW TO SPEAK
IN-N-OUT

At In-N-Out we say and do things a little differently. Common phrases you might hear at an In-N-Out store include the following:

Right-On

We often say "right-on" instead of "yes" or "okay." Saying "right-on" means, "I hear you and understand the instructions aimed at me." It's a positive form of agreement. Longtime associates affirm that this phrase has been around for many decades. It's a shortened form of a longer phrase like "right on the money" (accurate), "right on cue" (perfect timing), "right on the square" (perfectly measured), "right on target" (bull's-eye), and so on. This expression adds a positive emphasis to an idea. It can mean "cool" or "fantastic" or "you got it!"

Home Run

A home run is a car that reaches the drive-thru window without ordering at the speaker or with an associate in the drive lane. We don't find out the order until they reach the window. This phrase originated in the two-lane stores during the era when cooks took orders by memory. There were two lanes, one on either side of the kitchen. Two speakers were in each lane. When a cook missed taking an order, for whatever reason, the car would eventually get to the window, making it all the way home without having to stop at any of the other bases—they'd made a home run.

Lap Mat

The tradition of lap paper goes all the way back to the original Store Number 1. The first lap paper was the brown wax paper that our buns came wrapped in. Rather than throwing it away, Harry would cut the paper into smaller rectangles to hand out as lap paper. When buns started being packaged in plastic, Harry transitioned to pink butcher paper, which he had in supply from his meat department. Harry began printing lap mats in 1970. The first ones featured a map with the locations of the eight In-N-Out stores he had at the time, along with the name of the store manager at each store.

Walk-In

The walk-in is the large refrigerator that you can walk into as opposed to a reach-in refrigerator. Remember, we don't have any freezers. The temperature in a walk-in is between 34 and 41 degrees Fahrenheit.

Traulsen

Traulsen refers to the brand name of our first meat locker (where boxes of meat are kept). Over the years we've had other brands of meat lockers, but we still refer to them as the Traulsen. Like the walk-in, meat lockers are kept between 34 and 41 degrees.

The Salad Table/Board

The salad table is the area where burgers are dressed, wrapped, and packaged. It includes inserts with all of the products and ingredients needed. It's referred to as "the board" because of the thick wooden board where the burgers were dressed and wrapped. Today it is stainless steel.

Pomona Wrap

The paper we use to wrap the burgers is called Pomona Wrap. We would buy it in Pomona (Harry liked to do business with local vendors). It is also called menu tissue.

Insert

An insert is a stainless-steel container for storing our products, such as tomatoes and onions. Many other companies also refer to them as inserts. We do, too, because that's what Harry called them.

A Round

A round of something is just one of that type of item. This term is used when someone needs some of a product quickly or it's late at night and not too much of the product will be needed. This was a common practice in the old days when stores seldom closed with more than two associates. You didn't want to have tomatoes or onions left over, so you'd say, "Just slice me one round of tomato" or "one round onion" instead of one insert of tomato or onion.

Line-Up

This is the sheet associates consult prior to starting a shift to know what position they're working. In some of the older two-lane drive-thru stores where the back room is separate from the stand, a line-up is also used to describe a bucket of potatoes that has been peeled and cleaned and is ready to set out the door of the back room. The potato buckets were lined-up in order of rotation—an associate leaving the stand would get the first bucket in line but keep the order of the line-up, just like in baseball.

Relay

"Relay" is another baseball reference—when the throw is too long from the outfield to home, it is relayed using a cut-off person. When we're busy in the kitchen, the board person might not have time to get an order all the way where it needs to go (the fry table, a window, or the handout counter), so somebody needs to *relay* it there.

Counter Off

This is a term used to inform the counter handout associate (or whoever is free) that there's an order ready to be handed out (this will usually be called out by the Fry Person or the Board Person). Handing out the hot, ready-to-eat order right away is the first priority.

Drive Off

Same as above but for a drive order.

Lot Check

A lot check is when we make sure the lot is clean and free of trash. It's important to us that the interior and exterior of our stores are welcoming and clean. So we frequently perform lot checks to remove any trash or debris from our property.

Clearing the Car

This came from an aviation term, "to be clear for takeoff." A car in the drive lane is clear when the customer has been greeted, money has been taken, and lap mats and drinks have been given out. That car is cleared for takeoff—they only need their burgers and fries.

Snowed

This term is used when an associate is behind and requires help to get back on track. "Snowed" is a common restaurant term and not unique to In-N-Out. The word comes from the phrase "snowed under." Office workers started using the phrase when an overload of paperwork left their desks covered in white paper—snowed under. We simply shortened it to "snowed."

Insider Info #6

EVERYTHING YOU NEED TO KNOW ABOUT THE NOT-SO-SECRET MENU

How secret is our not-so-secret menu? You've heard the rumors, wondered what was on it, maybe even felt a little out of the loop. In reality, we don't have any secrets. It's just the way some of our customers like their burgers and fries prepared, and we're all about making our customers happy.

What follows are some of the most popular items on our not-so-secret menu. Note that some of these are listed on our website. Others you just have to hear about. Keep in mind that while all our associates are up to speed on our not-so-secret menu, every once in a while an order comes in that's highly unusual, so you might need to explain exactly what you'd like.

- **Animal Style.** The burger of your choice with lettuce, tomato, and a mustard-cooked beef patty; add pickle, extra spread, and grilled onions.

- **The Flying Dutchman.** Two slices of cheese melted between two burger patties. No buns. No veggies. (Harry was Dutch. This was his favorite snack. Guy's racing name was The Flying Dutchman.)

- **Protein Style.** Your favorite burger wrapped in hand-leafed lettuce instead of a bun.

- **Tomato Wrap.** Similar to a Protein Style, except tomatoes come where the buns usually are.

- **Grilled Cheese.** A grilled cheese sandwich is made with two slices of melted American cheese, lettuce, tomato, spread, with or without onions on a freshly toasted bun.

- **Double Meat.** Two 100 percent American beef patties, lettuce, tomato, spread, with or without onions.

- **3 x 3.** Also known as a Triple-Triple, it's three American beef patties, lettuce, tomato, spread, three slices of American cheese, with or without onions.

- **4 x 4.** Also known as a Quad-Quad, it's four 100 percent American beef patties, lettuce, tomato, spread, four slices of American cheese, with or without onions.

- **Buns.** You can request No Toast or Extra Toast.

- **Add chopped chilis.** Add some heat to your burger or fries.

- **Extra Everything.** Extra tomatoes, extra lettuce, extra onions, extra spread. This could be on a hamburger or on the side.

- **Cut in half or quarters.** For little kids, anyone who loves a smaller portion, or for sharing with a friend.

- **Cold cheese.** Some customers love their cheese unmelted.

- **Veggie Burger.** In days past this was sometimes referred to as a Wish Burger because customers wished there was a burger in it, although that expression isn't used as much anymore. Two buns piled with hand-leafed lettuce, sliced tomatoes, onions, spread, and pickles upon request. (To be clear, the Veggie Burger / Wish Burger doesn't contain an actual patty.)

- **Neapolitan.** Chocolate, vanilla, and strawberry milkshake, all in one cup but not swirled.

- **Black and White.** Chocolate and vanilla milkshake.

- **Root beer float.** Root beer and vanilla ice cream in a cup.

- **Well-done fries.** Extra crispy.

- **Cheese fries.** Just fries and cheese. Delicious.

- **In-N-Out stickers and paper hats.** Always free.

Insider Info #7

COLLECTIBLES AND
SPECIAL ITEMS

Good for One Burger:
The History of the In-N-Out Coin

Since ancient times coins have been the most universal embodiment of money. Maybe that's why Harry chose to make a burger coin instead of some sort of paper certificate. He grew up in an era when the value of the coin was in the metal it was made from rather than a representation of the value, as with paper money. Plus there's a certain satisfaction in having the solid weight of a real coin in your pocket. When Harry created his first burger coin in 1958, he made it large, about the size of a silver dollar. Borrowing from the formula of coins throughout history, he printed a simple declaration of the value of the coin on one side: *Good for One Burger*.

The creation of the burger coin helped to increase sales and build the brand. In 1958, Harry had only three stores. Inevitably, he would run into people who had never heard of In-N-Out Burger, let alone tried it. He wanted a way to tell them about the store. The genius of the burger coin is its tangibility; give someone a coupon printed on paper and they might lose it, tuck it away in a wallet or purse and forget about it, maybe send it through the laundry—you name it.

But a large coin doesn't go away, it doesn't fade, it serves as a constant reminder that you haven't spent it yet, and it reminds you of where, when, and how you acquired it. And potential customers were inclined to make that first visit to the store to spend that coin. From that point on, Harry hoped they'd be a customer for life.

The first Burger Coin was given out to associates and loyal customers in 1958. Each coin is good for one burger.

Six Fun Facts About the Burger Coin

1. **Menu Items Only.** The original coin declared *Good for One Burger.* Originally there were only hamburgers and cheeseburgers on the menu—the customer could choose either one. When the Double-Double was added to the menu, that "one burger" meant

the customer could opt for that as well. To this day, unless specifically spelled out otherwise, any promotional item is good for one
menu item.

2. **Full Price or No Charge.** Harry had such confidence in his
product and service that promotional items were always no
charge—the assumption being that once a customer tried our
products, the outstanding quality would bring them back and
create a customer for life. To this day we never provide coupons
or promotional discounts for any items. It's either full price or fully
on the house.

3. **No Expiration Date.** The burger coin didn't have an expiration
date. It was good for life—at any time and at any store. This started
a tradition where we always honor any burger promotion, regardless of any printed expiration date.

4. **Treat Every Customer like It's Their First Visit.** Harry told
his helpers to take really good care of customers with a burger coin
because it was most likely their first In-N-Out burger. Over time this
evolved into a tradition where we take care of *every* customer as if
it were their first visit—burger coin or not.

5. **Collectibility Keeps.** Any numismatist (coin collector) can tell
you that the coin saved will have more value than the coin spent.
Far more burger coins are issued than redeemed every year, so the
burger coin became the first item in a long list of In-N-Out collectibles that are sought after by customers and associates.

6. **Twelve Variations.** Over the years the look of the burger coin
has changed slightly (twelve variations have been made). One of
these variations included the creation of a twenty-dollar solid-silver
coin. But those are exceptionally rare—you must be promoted to
store manager to get one of the twenty-dollar coins.

History of In-N-Out Glassware
(1972–1984)

For twelve years Harry and Rich experimented with different marketing ideas toward building the In-N-Out brand. One of those initiatives was the sale of In-N-Out glassware.

1972: Pepsi "Tiffany" Glass

In 1972, In-N-Out still offered fountain soda in one size cup. Today this would be known as a small. The twelve-ounce soda sold for ten cents, but in 1972, In-N-Out offered a deal: you could purchase a sixteen-ounce "Tiffany" glass emblazoned with the Pepsi logo for twenty-five cents. We believe that we were the only restaurant chain to sell this glass, which could be purchased in a set of six via mail order through Pepsi for $2.95—double the cost and without the soda! We have learned that this glass was made by La Puente Glassworks. We think that Harry was able to purchase the glass directly from the local manufacturer, allowing him to bypass the middleman and sell the beautiful glass at a discount to In-N-Out customers. Pepsi was okay with this arrangement, as it meant their logo was filling America's cupboards.

1973–74: The Looney Tunes Series

The TV advertising for this series of eighteen glasses was provided by Pepsi, who created it in agreement with Warner Brothers Studio and advertised the glasses as "available at participating locations," with In-N-Out being the only local participant. The glasses sold for thirty cents and were the most successful glass we ever sold, owing in large part to the popularity of Looney Tunes.

Pepsi provided window placards to advertise the promotion and the glasses changed monthly. The full list of eighteen characters included Bugs Bunny, Sylvester, Tweety, Pepe Le Pew, Cool Cat, Henry Hawk, Elmer Fudd, Daffy Duck, Beaky Buzzard, Wile E. Coyote, Slow Poke Rodriguez,

Road Runner, Speedy Gonzalez, Porky Pig, Petunia Pig, Yosemite Sam, Tasmanian Devil, and Foghorn Leghorn.

1975: The "Uncola" Glass

7UP was one of the eight original drinks In-N-Out sold, but when we switched to fountain drinks in 1959 it was eliminated from our menu. In 1974, 7UP launched a marketing campaign touting 7UP as the Uncola. In 1975, when customers began asking for a caffeine-free soda option, Harry got permission from 7UP to sell the "upside down cola glass" shaped glass. An ad was placed in local papers informing customers that they could purchase the Uncola in the Uncola glass along with In-N-Out's "un-manufactured burgers."

1975: Bullwinkle and Friends Series

A licensing agreement to sell this series of glasses from August of 1975 somehow survived the warehouse fire. Pepsi made these glasses available for sale at "participating locations" as they had with the Looney Tunes series. *The Adventures of Rocky and Bullwinkle and Friends* was a popular television cartoon by Jay Ward Productions, an MGM subsidiary. Pepsi had negotiated with MGM to create these glasses using characters not just from the show also from Hanna Barbera Productions and MGM. Glasses were rotated monthly and included Bullwinkle, Rocky, Dudley Do-Right, Snidely Whiplash, and Tom & Jerry.

1977: Superhero Series

Pepsi provided another glass product with the Pepsi logo—a series of four long-standing superheroes in their updated 1970s costumes. The four super-heroes were Superman, Batman, Wonder Woman, and Aquaman. Unlike the prior glasses, the four were sold simultaneously at a price of fifty cents per glass (the small drink was now twenty cents). Since many stores still relied on memory rather than on written tags, the multiple options created some issues for the window hoppers when customers made multiple drink orders. For example, "Can I get a 7UP in a Superman glass, a root beer in a Batman glass, a Pepsi in an Aquaman glass, another Pepsi in a Superman glass, an orange soda in a Wonder Woman glass—oh, and a lemonade in a Batman glass?"

1977: In-N-Out Christmas Series

The Christmas glasses were the first to be produced and sold strictly for In-N-Out and, as a result, the first to be printed with our arrow logo. Besides a glass with Santa Claus carrying a sack full of hamburgers, there was a Christmas tree glass and a Rudolph the Red-Nosed Reindeer glass, both with In-N-Out themes. These glasses proved quite popular and sold well. While it's likely that the intention was to make this an annual event, when the warehouse fires occurred in 1978, that possibility was off the table for a while. To this day it is much harder to find samples of the Christmas glasses than most of the others.

1979: Sports Series

The final Pepsi-provided glass series was the sports-related themed glasses, and it proved to be short-lived. The artist, Gary Patterson, was an extremely successful comic-strip artist who created single-framed strips for the Sunday comics and sports magazines. Despite his popularity, the glasses did not sell well and In-N-Out discontinued selling them after a trial period of just a few months. Since this was a "participating locations" promo item, we can verify that some of our competitors were still trying to unload supplies as late as 1982.

1980–83: Christmas Glass

Like the 1977 series, this was a glass designed and produced specifically for In-N-Out with our logo, but like the "Tiffany" glass that started it all, this glass was also available in a gift box set of six. While this glass sold better than the sports series, it did not sell as well as the 1977 versions, perhaps because it was a single glass rather than a series. In 1983, a glass was produced with the same Santa Claus design but with a different, thinner-walled glass shape like the Indiana Jones glass. All preceding styles were tumbler glasses. This second glass was not as successful as the first and proved to be the last Christmas glass sold at our stores.

1984: Indiana Jones and the Temple of Doom Series

The first Indiana Jones movie was such an enormous success that In-N-Out partnered with 7UP to create this series of four glasses. Perhaps the "doom" in the movie title was prophetic—while popular at the box office, the movie was panned by critics. And the glasses? This set proved to be the least popular with our customers except for the sports series. It was the last glass we ever sold in our stores.

Have You Tried an In-N-Out Burger T-Shirt?

Of all the products we sell, the In-N-Out Burger T-shirt stands as unique for several reasons. It doesn't have a shelf life or an expiration date. It doesn't need rotation. Other than design, we have no hand in its creation. It's also the only product that differs from store to store, as some locations sell geographic-specific shirts.

Finally, while our other products have remained virtually unchanged since Harry and Esther started In-N-Out, the design of the T-shirt now changes at least once a year. All these factors make the T-shirt arguably the least In-N-Out-ish product we offer.

Even so, the In-N-Out T-shirt has become iconic—a walking billboard symbolizing everything In-N-Out represents, perhaps more than any other item we sell, except for our Double-Double.

Five Fun Facts About
In-N-Out Burger T-Shirts

1. **They started with Eddie the Butcher.** Harry got the idea for a T-shirt from Martin Edwards, aka Eddie the Butcher. In the early 1970s, Eddie drew a little cartoon character with the phrase "Eat Out at In 'N' Out" and printed it on sweatshirts (and later T-shirts) for his team who braved the cold temperatures of the meat department. He also sold these for two dollars to his friends who worked at In-N-Out stores. Bob Lang Sr. purchased one of these early sweatshirts and later donated it to In-N-Out Burger University upon his retirement. Eddie's creation was never sold to the public.

2. **Gumby Fry-Guy debuted in 1975.** When Harry saw his helpers wearing the T-shirts made by Eddie the Butcher, he liked the idea. In 1975, Harry designed the first official In-N-Out T-Shirt for sale in the stores. His design had a character nicknamed the "Gumby Fry-Guy" due to its resemblance to a Claymation character who was once a little green ball of clay. It is thought that Harry was trying to increase fry sales when he created the golden arrow–headed character.

3. **No flimsies.** Harry, as always, insisted on quality. He chose the Hanes Beefy-T as the platform for the new shirts, which were sold for two dollars.

4. **One size fits—some?** Originally, there was just one size: large. In the late 1970s, Rich added medium and X-large T-shirts, then small came later. It wasn't until after 1991, when the new Customer Service Line got us consistent feedback from our customers that a XX-large was needed and was soon added.

5. **The T-shirts led to love.** When my grandfather's health started failing in 1976, Guy was working at the warehouse, and he took over the job of outsourcing the T-Shirts. In the early 1980s, he met a graphic artist and salesperson named Lynda Lou Wilson, who asked why the In-N-Out shirts didn't represent the brand better. Guy suggested that she come up with a design. Over the next several weeks, Lynda showed several concepts to Guy, but he never bought one. Finally, Lynda confronted him and Guy used the opportunity to ask her on a date.

ACKNOWLEDGMENTS

THIS BOOK HAS BEEN SEVENTY-FIVE YEARS IN THE MAKING AND could not have been completed without the love, encouragement, hard work, and memories contributed by so many who have come before me and continue to walk beside me in this journey.

To my loved ones who paved the way for the amazing company and my In-N-Out family: Grandpa, Grams, Uncle Richie, and Dad—I am so grateful for your vision, values, and leadership. I miss you every day! Though you may no longer be physically in my life, your love and memories are forever held in my heart. I pray this book is one more way I can carry on your legacy with the highest levels of quality and service.

To my family members who continue to encourage me every single day and helped guide me in how to share both the painful and joyous memories of our shared story: my mom, Lynda, and my sisters, Teri and Traci—I'm so blessed to have such incredible and strong women in my life and am grateful to have you by my side. My brother-in-law, co-worker, and friend, Mark Taylor, I love and appreciate you more than words can ever express. Most of all, my husband Sean, thank you for putting up with my late nights of writing and editing. You are my best friend and the love of my life. There is no one else I'd rather go through this life with. You are my well outside of heaven, and I am grateful for you every day and love our adventures.

To all the amazing and hardworking In-N-Out Associates both past and present: I want you all to know how special you are. I'm beyond grateful for the huge amounts of time, knowledge, and memories you shared to make this book a reality. This book is stronger because of you: Wendell Ansnes, Dean Atkins, Keith Brazeau, Tom Evans, Greg Fairchild, Joe Gee, Todd Gorton, Jeff Helmrich, Ken Iriart, Roger Kotch, Bob Lang Jr., Bob Lang Sr., Jodie Medlock, Ray Maldonado, Rudy Mercado, Tom Moon, Gary Murphy, Chuck Papez, Ed Pendleton, Jon Peterson, Jack Ruley, Bill Scherer, Donna Turkmani, and Carl Van Fleet.

To the best leadership team there is, our In-N-Out VPs: Mike Abbate, George Charlesworth, Mike Cowan, Alex Frumusanu, Rob Howards, Mike Mravle, Katie Sauls, Arnie Wensinger and, in particular, Denny Warnick, whose incredible leadership and historical expertise helped bring together decades of facts and associates who contributed to this book.

To the associates who continually support and assist me: Michaella Abell, Verenice Millan, and Peyton Russell—thank you for keeping me on track and organized. Seriously, I couldn't do it without you ladies.

To the entire In-N-Out marketing team: Jen Atwater, Gregg Barnard, Jiin Billings, Cassie Brodowski, William Burroughs, Jeff Dreher, Kathleen Hardesty, Taylor Harkins, Caitlin Holliday, Melissa Noriega, Cody Ogg, and Kyrie Woodring. I am forever grateful for your passion and expertise.

To the rock star team outside of my In-N-Out family that helped bring this book to life: My literary agent, Tom Dean, thank you for taking such great care of this story and legacy. Ami McConnell and Marcus Brotherton, thank you for so beautifully capturing my words and heart. The HarperCollins publishing team, Brigitta Nortker, Janet Talbert, Kristen Golden, and Lisa Beech, thank you for helping to share this story with the world. My publicist, Kristin Cole, I'm grateful for all that you do. Love you, girl.

Lastly, I want to thank In-N-Out's most important asset, our guests: the customers! You are our #1 and the reason we exist. This book would not exist without your loyal support through the last seventy-five years! We work for you and love serving you.

Finally, to the One who deserves all the glory: God. I am in awe of the blessings he has bestowed upon In-N-Out and me, and am forever grateful for the strength, protection, and unconditional love he provides me every single day. You have carried both the company and me through tough times, and we have gone against the odds and made it seventy-five years strong because of you!

NOTES

Chapter 2: One Small Hamburger Stand

1. "Harry Snyder," World War II Army Enlistment Records, 1938–46.
2. Bob Lang Sr., interview with In-N-Out researcher, 2022.

Chapter 3: A Driving Pace

1. Tom Evans, interview with In-N-Out researcher, 2022.
2. Esther Snyder, video recording, In-N-Out archives.
3. Tom Cassini, interview with In-N-Out researcher, 2022.
4. Joe Gee (longtime associate), interview with In-N-Out researcher, 2022.
5. Bob Ruley, interview with In-N-Out researcher, 2022.
6. Joe Gee, interview with In-N-Out researcher, 2022.

Chapter 4: Redemption

1. Ed Pendleton, interview with In-N-Out researcher, 2022.
2. To book an In-N-Out Cookout Truck, call 1-800-700-7774 or visit https://www.In-N-Out.com/cookout.
3. Jeff Helmrich, interview with In-N-Out researcher, 2022.
4. Cindy W. Christian, "Child Abuse and Neglect: Introduction," *New England Journal of Medicine*, last updated April 2022, https://resident360.nejm.org /rotation-prep/child-abuse-and-neglect/introduction.

Chapter 5: The Era of Uncle Rich

1. Esther Snyder on BTV, In-N-Out Archives.
2. Ray Maldonado, interview with In-N-Out researcher, 2022.
3. Mark Taylor, interview with In-N-Out researcher, 2022.
4. Bob Lang Jr., interview with In-N-Out researcher, 2022.
5. "Obituary: Sarah Margaret Courtney, 1924–2019," Starbuck-Lind Mortuary, September 8, 2019, https://www.starbucklind.com/obituary/sarah-courtney.

Chapter 6: Open Doors and Lots of Growth

1. Lynda Snyder, interview with In-N-Out researcher, 2022.
2. Greg Hernandez, "In-N-Out Executive's Death Ruled Accidental," *Los Angeles Times*, January 26, 2000, https://www.latimes.com/archives/la-xpm-2000-jan-26-fi-57713-story.html.
3. Bill Scherer, interview with In-N-Out researcher, 2022.
4. Esther Snyder, interview with In-N-Out researcher, 2022.

Chapter 7: The Worst Night of Our Lives

1. John Peterson, interview with In-N-Out researcher, 2022.
2. Ed Pendleton, interview with In-N-Out researcher, 2022. Ed also noted, "It was really Diane's idea for me to tell Rich about it."
3. Bob Lang Sr., interview with In-N-Out researcher, 2022.
4. Camel story from John Peterson, interview with In-N-Out researcher, 2022.
5. Rich Snyder on BTV, In-N-Out Archives.
6. Rebecca Trounson and Jeffrey A. Perlman, "Crash That Killed In-N-Out Officers Is Investigated," *Los Angeles Times*, December 17, 1993, https://www.latimes.com/archives/la-xpm-1993-12-17-mn-2813-story.html.
7. Information from In-N-Out historian, 2022.
8. Rebecca Trounson and Greg Johnson, "2 Executives of In-N-Out Chain Died in Crash," *Los Angeles Times*, December 17, 1993, https://www.latimes.com/archives/la-xpm-1993-12-17-mn-2639-story.html.
9. Keith Brazeau, interview with In-N-Out researcher, 2022.
10. Donna Turkmani, interview with In-N-Out researcher, 2022.
11. Bill Scherer, interview with In-N-Out researcher, 2022.

Chapter 8: Guy at the Wheel

1. Guy Snyder on BTV, In-N-Out Archives.
2. Guy Snyder on BTV, In-N-Out Archives.
3. Guy Snyder on BTV, In-N-Out Archives.

4. Guy Snyder on BTV, In-N-Out Archives.

5. Wendell Ansnes, interview with In-N-Out researcher, 2022.

6. Guy Snyder on BTV, In-N-Out Archives.

7. Guy Snyder on BTV, In-N-Out Archives.

8. Guy Snyder on BTV, In-N-Out Archives.

9. Bill Scherer, interview with In-N-Out researcher, 2022.

10. In-N-Out archives.

11. Jeff Helmrich, interview with In-N-Out researcher, 2022.

12. Lynda Snyder, interview with In-N-Out researcher, 2022.

13. Mayo Clinic Staff, "Porphyria," Mayo Clinic, April 5, 2023, https://www
.mayoclinic.org/diseases-conditions/porphyria/symptoms-causes/syc-20356066.

14. Guy Snyder, BTV, In-N-Out Archives.

15. Greg Hernandez, "In-N-Out Executive's Death Ruled Accidental," *Los Angeles
Times*, January 26, 2000, https://www.latimes.com/archives/la-xpm-2000-jan-26
-fi-57713-story.html.

Chapter 9: Esther's Team

1. Greg Fairchild, interview with In-N-Out researcher, 2022.

2. Donna Turkmani, interview with In-N-Out researcher, 2022.

3. "Esther Snyder, In-N-Out Burger Founder, Dies at 86," *New York Times*,
August 13, 2006, https://www.nytimes.com/2006/08/13/business/13snyder.html.

4. Myrna Oliver, "Esther Snyder, 86; Co-Founded the In-N-Out Burger Chain,"
Los Angeles Times, August 6, 2012, https://www.latimes.com/archives/la-xpm
-2006-aug-06-me-snyder6-story.html.

5. Stephen Miller, "Family Affair: End of an Era at a Cult Chain," *Wall Street Journal*,
August 12, 2006, https://www.wsj.com/articles/SB115534920190234107.

Chapter 10: The Third Generation

1. Information from the National Human Trafficking Hotline and Human
Trafficking Search, cited at "Human Trafficking," Slave 2 Nothing, accessed
May 24, 2023, https://www.slave2nothing.org/human-trafficking. See also
the Polaris Project at https://polarisproject.org/human-trafficking/.

2. For more information about our efforts, see Slave 2 Nothing: www.slave2nothing.org.

3. For more information, please see Army of Love: https://armyoflove.com.

Insider Info #1

1. "California Transparency in Supply Chain," In-N-Out Burger, accessed
May 25, 2023, https://www.In-N-Out.com/ca-transparency-supply-chain.

ABOUT THE AUTHOR

FROM THE DAY LYNSI SNYDER-ELLINGSON WAS BORN IN SOUTHERN California in 1982, In-N-Out Burger has been a significant part of her life. Her grandparents, Harry and Esther Snyder, founded In-N-Out Burger in 1948, and to this day the business remains privately owned and operated. In-N-Out Burger has always been a family business, and Lynsi intends to keep it that way.

She began working as an associate at In-N-Out Burger in 1999. She is currently the owner and president of the company and continues to be deeply involved with every aspect of the business—including daily operations, marketing, merchandising, event planning, associate engagement, company expansion, culture, training, designing stores, and more.

Lynsi is a visionary and servant leader committed to maintaining and enhancing the well-being of the entire In-N-Out Burger family, which now numbers approximately 38,000 associates. Additionally, she directs and helps to oversee all of In-N-Out Burger's philanthropic efforts through the In-N-Out Burger Foundation, which was started by her Grandma Esther and Uncle Rich, and the Slave 2 Nothing Foundation, which was started by Lynsi and her husband, Sean Ellingson.

Lynsi and Sean are also the founders and visionaries for Army of Love, a nonprofit organization that exists for the purpose of uniting the body of Christ through training tools that will set them free to set others free. Army of Love strives to exemplify Isaiah 61:1: "The Spirit of the Lord GOD is upon Me, because the Lord has anointed Me to preach good tidings to the poor; He has sent Me to heal the brokenhearted, to proclaim liberty to the captives, and the opening of the prison to those who are bound."

In addition to God being on the throne of her heart, Lynsi is a devoted wife and proud mother of four beautiful children. She strives to balance the many responsibilities on her plate and to be a good steward of what she has been given. Her goal is to be the type of person described in Proverbs 31.